D0852692

Issues of Our Time

Ours has been called an information age, but, though information has never been more plentiful, ideas are what shape and reshape our world. "Issues of Our Time" is a series of books in which some of today's leading thinkers explore ideas that matter in the new millennium. The authors—including the philosopher Kwame Anthony Appiah, the sociologist William Julius Wilson, the social psychologist Claude Steele, the legal scholars Charles Fried and Alan Dershowitz, the Pulitzer Prize–winning critic Louis Menand, and the Nobel Prize–winning economist Amartya Sen—honor clarity without shying away from complexity; these books are both genuinely engaged and genuinely engaging. Each recognizes the importance not just of our values but also of the way we resolve the conflicts among those values. Law, justice, identity, morality, and freedom: concepts such as these are at once abstract and utterly close to home. Our understanding of them helps define who we are and who we hope to be; we are made by what we make of them. These are books, accordingly, that invite the reader to reexamine hand-me-down assumptions and to grapple with powerful trends. Whether you are moved to reason together with these authors, or to argue with them, they are sure to leave your views tested, if not changed. The perspectives of the authors in this series are diverse, the voices are distinctive, the issues are vital.

HENRY LOUIS GATES JR., SERIES EDITOR
W. E. B. DU BOIS PROFESSOR OF THE HUMANITIES
HARVARD UNIVERSITY

Issues of Our Time

Other titles

KWAME ANTHONY APPIAH
Cosmopolitanism

AMARTYA SEN
Identity and Violence: The Illusion of Destiny

ALAN DERSHOWITZ
Preemption: A Knife That Cuts Both Ways

CHARLES FRIED
Modern Liberty and the Limits of Government

WILLIAM JULIUS WILSON
More Than Just Race

LOUIS MENAND
The Marketplace of Ideas

Forthcoming authors

AMY GUTMANN
NICHOLAS LEMANN

WHISTLING VIVALDI

AND OTHER CLUES TO HOW STEREOTYPES AFFECT US

Claude M. Steele

W. W. NORTON & COMPANY
NEW YORK • LONDON

Copyright © 2010 by Claude M. Steele

All rights reserved
Printed in the United States of America
First Edition

For information about permission to reproduce selections from this book,
write to Permissions, W. W. Norton & Company, Inc.,
500 Fifth Avenue, New York, NY 10110

For information about special discounts for bulk purchases, please contact
W. W. Norton Special Sales at specialsales@wwnorton.com or 800-233-4830

Manufacturing by RR Donnelley Bloomsburg

Library of Congress Cataloging-in-Publication Data

Steele, Claude.
   Whistling Vivaldi : and other clues to how stereotypes affect us /
Claude M. Steele.—1st ed.
      p. cm. — (Issues of our time)
   Includes bibliographical references and index.
   ISBN 978-0-393-06249-6 (hbk.)
1. Stereotypes (Social psychology) 2. Group identity. 3. Discrimination.
I. Title.
   HM1096.S736 2010
   303.3'85—dc22

                                                      2009052079

W. W. Norton & Company, Inc.
500 Fifth Avenue, New York, N.Y. 10110
www.wwnorton.com

W. W. Norton & Company Ltd.
Castle House, 75/76 Wells Street, London W1T 3QT

1 2 3 4 5 6 7 8 9 0

*To Dorothy and, in order of their arrival in the clan,
Jory, Ben, Dayna, Sidney, Coleman, and Matthew*

And to my parents, Ruth and Shelby Steele

CONTENTS

Acknowledgments xi

CHAPTER 1 *An Introduction: At the Root of Identity* 1

CHAPTER 2 *A Mysterious Link Between Identity and Intellectual Performance* 16

CHAPTER 3 *Stereotype Threat Comes to Light, and in More than One Group* 44

CHAPTER 4 *A Broader View of Identity: In the Lives of Anatole Broyard, Amin Maalouf, and the Rest of Us* 63

CHAPTER 5 *The Many Experiences of Stereotype Threat* 85

CHAPTER 6 *Identity Threat and the Efforting Life* 99

CHAPTER 7 *The Mind on Stereotype Threat: Racing and Overloaded* 114

CHAPTER 8 *The Strength of Stereotype Threat: The Role of Cues* 134

CHAPTER 9 *Reducing Identity and Stereotype Threat: A New Hope* 152

CHAPTER 10 *The Distance Between Us: The Role of Identity Threat* 191

CHAPTER 11 *Conclusion: Identity as a Bridge Between Us* 211

References 220

Index 231

ACKNOWLEDGMENTS

Despite my protest that psychologists write articles not books, Skip Gates and Roby Harrington persisted in encouraging me to write this book and for that I thank them. I also thank them for the support and patience they showed me during the writing of the book—and for the idea of this book series.

Social psychological research is a collaborative enterprise, and the collaborations at the core of my research provide the narrative structure of this book. Thus many collaborators are described throughout its pages (many of whom were also commentators on sections of this book). But some collaborators whose research did not wind up in the book, but who nonetheless importantly influenced my research and thinking, are Priyanka Carr, Emily Pronin, Daryl Wout, Julie Garcia, and David Sherman.

I also want to extend special thanks to Hazel Markus and to the late Robert Zajonc, whose friendship, support, and constant willingness to engage the ideas of this work and add insight to it made this book far better than it would otherwise have been. Thanks go also to their daughter, Krysia Zajonc, whose forthcoming and honest relaying of her experiences in college contributed importantly to the book. It is also worth noting that scientists are people too, and the support of friends and colleagues like Ewart Thomas, Jennifer Eberhardt, Carol Dweck, Lee Ross, Mark Lepper, Dale Miller, Larry Bobo, Marcy Morgan, and my colleagues at Stanford's Center for the Comparative Study in Race and Ethnicity made this work, again, better than it would have been. Also, Keith Wailoo and Richard Nisbett provided very useful comments on early chapters of the book. I offer these appreciations but stress that none of these good people have any responsibility for the errors or errant judgments that you, the reader, may encounter.

I am also grateful to my editors at W. W. Norton—Mollie Eisenberg, Jake Schindel, and, again, Roby Harrington—for their thoughtful, often revealing comments that helped every aspect of this book and that gently pushed and guided me to make it better. Similar thanks go to several people who, as student research assistants, helped me with various aspects of preparing the manuscript: Hilary Bergsieker, Matthew Jackson, and especially April House, who did such a thoughtful job collecting references in the final stages of preparing the manuscript. Special thanks as well to my agent, Tina Bennett, for making the whole process a smooth and enjoyable one.

Research requires the beneficence of funders, and for the beneficence that enabled my own research reported in this book I will always be grateful to the National Institute of Mental Health for several research grants, and especially to the Russell Sage Foundation and its president, Eric Wanner, who early on was willing to take a chance with this research and, by sticking with it, allowed it to develop into a mature contribution.

Finally, I would like to thank my colleagues at the Center for Advanced Study in the Behavioral Sciences at Stanford, who were blessedly tolerant of me neglecting my director's duties long enough to bring this book to a conclusion. Patience is the milk of human kindness, and they are indeed a kind group of friends and colleagues.

Whistling Vivaldi

CHAPTER 1

─■─

An Introduction: At the Root of Identity

1.

I have a memory of the first time I realized I was black. It was when, at seven or eight, I was walking home from school with neighborhood kids on the last day of the school year—the whole summer in front of us—and I learned that we "black" kids couldn't swim at the pool in our area park, except on Wednesday afternoons. And then on those summer Wednesdays, with our swimming suits wrapped tightly in our towels, we filed, caravan-style, out of our neighborhood toward the hallowed pool in the adjoining white neighborhood. It was a strange weekly pilgrimage. It marked the racial order of the time and place—Chicagoland, the 1950s and early 1960s. For me it was what the psychologist William Cross calls an "encounter"—with the very fact that there was a racial order. The implications of this order for my life seemed massive—a life of swimming only on Wednesday afternoons? Why? Moreover, it turned out to be a portent of things to come. I next found out that we black kids—who, by the way, lived in my neighborhood and who had been, until these encounters, just kids—couldn't go to the roller rink, except on Thursday nights. We could be regular people but only in the middle of the week? These segregations were hard to ignore. And mistakes were costly, as when, at thirteen, after arriving at six in the morning, I waited all day to be hired as a caddy at an area golf course, only to be told at the end of the day that they didn't hire Negroes. This is how I became aware I was black. I didn't know what being black meant, but I was getting the idea that it was a big deal.

With decades of hindsight, I now think I know what was going on. I was recognizing nothing less than a condition of life—most important, a condition of life tied to my race, to my being black in that time and place. The condition was simple enough: *if* I joined the caravan and went to the pool on Wednesday afternoons *then* I got in; *if* I went to the pool any other time, *then* I didn't get in. To my seven- or eight-year-old self, this was a bad condition of life. But the condition itself wasn't the worst of it. For example, had my parents imposed it on me for not taking out the garbage, I wouldn't have been so upset. What got me was that it was imposed on me because I was black. There was nothing I could do about that, and if being black was reason enough to restrict my swimming, then what else would happen because of it?

In an interview many years later, a college student, whom you will meet later in this book, would describe for me an experience that took a similar form. He was one of only two whites in an African American political science class composed of mostly black and other minority students. He, too, described a condition of life: if he said something that revealed an ignorance of African American experience, or a confusion about how to think about it, then he could well be seen as racially insensitive, or . . . worse; if he said nothing in class, then he could largely escape the suspicion of his fellow students. His condition, like my swimming pool condition, made him feel his racial identity, his whiteness, in that time and place—something he hadn't thought much about before.

From experiences like these, troubling questions arise. Will there be other conditions? How many? In how many areas of life? Will they be about important things? Can you avoid them? Do you have to stay on the lookout for them?

When I encountered my swimming pool restriction, it mystified me. Where did it come from? Conditions of life tied to identity like that still mystify me. But now I have a working idea about where they come from. They come from the way a society, at a given time, is organized around an identity like race. That organization reflects the history of a place, as well as the ongoing individual and group competition for opportunity and the good life. The way Chicagoland was organized around race in the late 1950s and early 1960s—the rigid housing segregation, the de facto school segregation, the employment discrimination, and so on—meant that black people in that time and place had many restrictive conditions of life tied to their identity, perhaps the least of which was the Wednesday afternoon swimming restriction that so worried my seven- or eight-year-old self.

This book is about what my colleagues and I call *identity contingencies*—the things you have to deal with in a situation because you have a given social identity, because you are old, young, gay, a white male, a woman, black, Latino, politically conservative or liberal, diagnosed with bipolar disorder, a cancer patient, and so on. Generally speaking, contingencies are circumstances you have to deal with in order to get what you want or need in a situation. In the Chicagoland of my youth, in order to go swimming I had to restrict my pool going to Wednesday afternoons. That's a contingency. In his African American political science class, my interviewee had the added pressure that his ignorance could cause him serious disapproval. That, too, is a contingency. What makes both of these contingencies identity contingencies is that the people involved had to deal with them because they had a particular social identity in the situation. Other people in the situation didn't have to deal with them, just the people who had the same identity he had. This book examines the role these *identity contingencies* play in our lives, in the broader society, and in some of society's most tenacious problems.

Now, of course, ours is an individualistic society. We don't like to think that conditions tied to our social identities have much say in our lives, especially if we don't want them to. We have a creed. When barriers arise, we're supposed to march through the storm, picking ourselves up by our bootstraps. I have to count myself a subscriber to this creed. But this book offers an important qualification to this creed: that by imposing on us certain conditions of life, our social identities can strongly affect things as important as our performances in the classroom and on standardized tests, our memory capacity, our athletic performance, the pressure we feel to prove ourselves, even the comfort level we have with people of different groups—all things we typically think of as being determined by individual talents, motivations, and preferences.

The purpose of this book is nothing less than to bring this poorly understood part of social reality into view. I hope to convince you that ignoring it—allowing our creed of individualism, for example, to push it into the shadows—is costly, to our own personal success and development, to the quality of life in an identity-diverse society and world, and to our ability to fix some of the bad ways that identity still influences the distribution of outcomes in society.

How do identity contingencies influence us? Some constrain our behavior down on the ground, like restricted access to a public swimming pool. Others, just as powerful, influence us more subtly, not by constraining behavior on the ground but by putting a threat in the air.

2.

At the center of this book is a particular kind of identity contingency, that of stereotype threat. I believe stereotype threat is a standard predicament of life. It springs from our human powers of intersubjectivity—the fact that as members of society we have a pretty good idea of what other members of our society think about lots of things, including the major groups and identities in society. We could all take out a piece of paper, write down the major stereotypes of these identities, and show a high degree of agreement in what we wrote. This means that whenever we're in a situation where a bad stereotype about one of our own identities could be applied to us—such as those about being old, poor, rich, or female—we know it. We know what "people could think." We know that anything we do that fits the stereotype could be taken as confirming it. And we know that, for that reason, we could be judged and treated accordingly. That's why I think it's a standard human predicament. In one form or another—be it through the threat of a stereotype about having lost memory capacity or being cold in relations with others—it happens to us all, perhaps several times a day.

It is also a threat that, like the swimming pool restriction, is tied to an identity. It is present in any situation to which the stereotype is relevant. And this means that it follows members of the stereotyped group into these situations like a balloon over their heads. It can be very hard to shake.

Consider the experience of Brent Staples, now a columnist for the *New York Times*, but then a psychology graduate student at the University of Chicago, a young African American male dressed in informal student clothing walking down the streets of Chicago's Hyde Park neighborhood. In his own words:

> I became an expert in the language of fear. Couples locked arms or reached for each other's hand when they saw me. Some crossed to the other side of the street. People who were carrying on conversations went mute and stared straight ahead, as though avoiding my eyes would save them. . . .
>
> I'd been a fool. I'd been walking the streets grinning good evening at people who were frightened to death of me. I did violence to them by just being. How had I missed this . . .
>
> I tried to be innocuous but didn't know how. . . . I began to avoid people. I turned out of my way into side streets to spare them the sense that they were being stalked. . . . Out of nervousness I began to whistle and discovered I was good at it. My whistle was pure and sweet—and also in tune. On the street at night I whistled popular tunes from the Beatles and Vivaldi's *Four Seasons*. The tension drained from people's bodies when they heard me. A few even smiled as they passed me in the dark. (pp. 202–3)

Staples was dealing with a phantom, a bad stereotype about his race that was in the air on the streets of Hyde Park—the stereotype that young African American males in this neighborhood are violence prone. People from other groups in other situations might face very different stereotypes—about lacking math ability rather than being violence prone for example—but their predicaments would be the same. When they were in situations where those stereotypes could apply to them, they understood that one false move could cause them to be reduced to that stereotype, to be seen and treated in terms of it. That's stereotype threat, a contingency of their identity in these situations.

Unless, as Staples discovered, they devised a way to deflect it. Staples whistled Vivaldi, by his own account a very good version of it. What would that do for him? Would it improve his attitude toward others on the street, make him more understanding? Probably not. What it did for sure was change the situation he was dealing with. And how it did this illustrates nicely the nature of stereotype threat. In a single stroke, he made the stereotype about violence-prone African American males less applicable to him personally. He displayed knowledge of white culture, even "high white culture." People on the street may not have recognized the Vivaldi he was whistling, but they could tell he was whistling classical music. This caused him to be seen differently, as an educated, refined person, not as a violence-prone African American youth. Such youths don't typically walk down the street whistling classical music. While hardly being aware of it, people drop the stereotype of violence-proneness as the lens through which they see him. He seems less threatening. People don't know who he is; but they know he isn't someone to fear. Fear fades from their demeanor. Staples himself relaxes. The stereotype in the air that threatened him is fended off. And the change in the behavior of those on the street, and in his own behavior, reveals the power that a mere stereotype—floating in the air like a cloud gathering the nation's history—was having on everyone all along.

Whistling Vivaldi is about the experience of living under such a cloud—an experience we all have—and the role such clouds play in shaping our lives and society.

3.

Suppose you are invited into a psychology laboratory and asked to play ten holes of golf on a miniature course that has been set up in a small room. Suppose also that you are a white college student, reasonably athletically inclined. Now suppose that just as you are getting the feel of the golf clubs, you are told that the golf task is part of a standardized sports psychology measure called the Michigan Athletic Aptitude Test (MAAT), which measures "natural athletic ability." How well do you think you'd do? Would being told that the golf task measures natural athletic ability make a difference?

A group of social psychologists at Princeton University led by Jeff Stone did exactly this experiment several years ago. They found something very interesting: white students who were told the golf task measured natural athletic ability golfed a lot worse than white students who were told nothing about the task. They tried just as hard. But it took them, on average, three strokes more to get through the course.

What was it about thinking of the task as a measure of natural athletic ability that so strikingly undermined their performance?

Jeff and his colleagues reasoned that it had something to do with their being white. In the terms I have been using, it had to do with a contingency of white identity that comes to bear in situations where natural athletic ability is being evaluated. This contingency comes from a broadly known stereotype in this society that, compared with blacks at least, whites may have less natural athletic ability. Participants in Jeff's experiment would know this stereotype simply by being members of this society. They might not believe it. But being told that the golfing task measured the very trait their group was stereotyped as lacking, just before they began the task, could put them in a quandary: their frustration on the task could be seen as confirming the stereotype, as a characterization both of themselves and of their group. And this, in turn, might be upsetting and distracting enough to add an average of three strokes to their scores.

The stereotype about their group, and the threatening interpretation of their golf frustration that it posed, is not a contingency like the swimming pool restriction of my youth that directly affected behavior. It imposed no extra restrictions on their golfing, or any material impediments. But it was nonetheless a contingency of their identity during the golf task. If they experienced frustration at golf, *then* they could be confirming, or be seen to be confirming, the unsavory stereotype. If they didn't experience frustration at golf, *then* they didn't confirm the racial stereotype. This was an extra pressure they had to deal with during the golfing task, for no other reason than that they were white. It hung over them as a threat in the air, implying that one false move could get them judged and treated as a white kid with no natural athletic ability. (You will learn later in the book how my colleagues and I came to call this kind of threat in the air simply *stereotype threat*.)

With this reasoning in tow, Jeff and colleagues started asking more questions.

If the mere act of telling white Princeton students that their golfing measured natural athletic ability had caused them to golf poorly by distracting them with the risk of being stereotyped, then telling black Princeton students the same thing should have no effect on their golfing, since their group isn't stereotyped in that way. And it didn't. Jeff and his colleagues had put a group of black Princeton students through the same procedure they'd put the white students through. And, lo and behold, their golfing was unaffected. They golfed the same whether or not they'd been told the task measured natural athletic ability.

Here was more evidence that what had interfered with white students' golfing, when it was seen to measure natural athletic ability, was a distracting sense of threat arising from how whites are stereotyped in the larger society.

But Jeff and his research team weren't satisfied. They devised a still cleverer way to make their argument.

They reasoned that if group stereotypes can really set up threats in the air that are capable of interfering with actions as concrete as golfing for entire groups of people—like the stereotype threat Staples had to contend with on the streets of Hyde Park—then it should be possible to set up a stereotype threat that would interfere with black students' golfing as well. All they'd have to do was represent the golfing task as measuring something related to a bad stereotype of blacks. Then, as black participants golfed, they'd have to fend off, like whites in the earlier experiment, the bad stereotype about their group. This added pressure might hurt their golfing.

They tested this idea in a simple way. They told new groups of black and white Princeton students that the golf task they were about to begin was a measure of "sports strategic intelligence." This simple change of phrase had a powerful effect. It now put black students at risk, through their golfing, of confirming or being seen to confirm the ancient and very bad stereotype of blacks as less intelligent. Now, as they tried to sink their putts, any mistake could make them feel vulnerable to being judged and treated like a less intelligent black kid. That was a heavy contingency of identity in this situation indeed, which might well cause enough distraction to interfere with their golfing. Importantly, this same instruction freed white students of stereotype threat in this situation, since whites aren't stereotyped as less intelligent.

The results were dramatic. Now the black students, suffering their form of stereotype threat during the golfing task, golfed dramatically worse than the white students, for whom this instruction had lifted stereotype threat. They took, on average, four strokes more to get through the course.

Neither whites, when the golfing task was represented as a test of natural athletic ability, nor blacks, when it was represented as a test of sports strategic intelligence, confronted a directly interfering contingency of identity in these experiments—nothing that directly affected their behavior like a swimming pool restriction. The contingencies they faced were threats in the air—the threat that their golfing could confirm or be seen to confirm a bad group stereotype as a characterization of their group and of themselves. Still, it was a threat with a big effect. On a course that typically took between twenty-two and twenty-four strokes to complete, it led whites to take three more strokes to complete it, and blacks to take five more strokes to complete it.

At first glance, one might dismiss the importance of something "in the air" like stereotype threat. At second glance, however, it's clear that this threat can be a tenacious force in our lives. Staples had to contend with it every time he walked down the streets of his own neighborhood. White athletes have to contend with it in each competition, especially against black athletes. Think of the white athlete in a sport with heavy black competition. To reach a high level of performance, say, to make it into the National Basketball Association, which is dominated by black players, the white athlete would have to survive and prosper against a lifelong gauntlet of performance situations loaded with this extra race-linked threat. No single good athletic performance would put the stereotype to rest. The effort to disprove it would be Sisyphean, reemergent at each important new performance.

The aim of this book is not to show that stereotype threat is so powerful and persistent that it can't be overcome. Quite the contrary. Its goal is to show how, as an unrecognized factor in our lives, it can contribute to some of our most vexing personal and societal problems, but that doing quite feasible things to reduce this threat can lead to dramatic improvements in these problems.

4.

Now suppose it wasn't miniature golf that you were asked to perform when you arrived at a psychology experiment, and suppose it
wasn't your group's athletic ability that was negatively stereotyped
in the larger society. Suppose it was difficult math problems that
you were asked to solve on a timed standardized test, and suppose
that it was your group's math ability that was negatively stereotyped in the larger society. In other words, suppose you were an
American woman showing up for an experiment involving difficult
math.

Would the stereotype threat that is a contingency of your gender
identity in math-related settings be enough to interfere with your
performance on the test? Would you be able to just push through
this threat of being seen stereotypically and perform well anyway?
Or would the very effort to push hard on a timed test be distracting enough to impair your performance despite the extra effort?
Would you experience this threat, this contingency of identity,
every time you tried difficult math in settings with males around?
Would this contingency of identity in math settings become frustrating enough to make you avoid math-related college majors and
careers? Would women living in a society where women's math
ability is not negatively stereotyped experience this threat? Would
their scores be better?

Or suppose the test you were asked to take wasn't the Michigan
Athletic Aptitude Test but was the SAT, and suppose the negative
stereotype about your group wasn't about athletic ability, or even
about math ability, alone, but about scholastic ability in general.
Again, would the stereotype threat you experience as a contingency of your identity in scholastic settings be enough to interfere
with your performance on this test? Does the threat cause this

interference by diverting mental resources away from the test and onto your worries? Would the stereotype threat you experience in scholastic settings affect other experiences as well, such as your classroom performance and your comfort interacting with teachers, professors, teaching assistants, and even other students not in your group? Would this contingency of identity make these settings so frustrating for you that you might try to avoid them in choosing a walk of life?

The purpose of this book is to describe the journey that my colleagues and I have taken in formulating these and related questions and then in systematically trying to answer them over the past twenty years. The experience has been like trying to solve a mystery. And the approach of the book is to give you an over-the-shoulder view of how that mystery has unfolded, of the progression of ideas and revelations, often from the research itself, about the surprising ways that stereotypes affect us—our intellectual functioning, our stress reactions, the tension that can exist between people from different groups, and the sometimes very surprising strategies that alleviate these effects and thereby help solve some of society's worst problems. And because science is rarely a solitary activity anymore—something long true for me—the story also describes many of the people who have done this research, as well as how they work. You will also meet many interesting people who have experienced this threat—including a famous journalist, an African American expatriate in Paris, a person who rose from sharecropping to wealth in rural North Carolina, students at some of America's most elite universities, and students in some of America's most wanting K through 12 schools.

Although the book deals with issues that can have a political charge, neither it nor the work it reports is propelled by an ideological orientation—to the best of my and my colleagues' ability. One of the first things one learns as a social psychologist is that everyone is capable of bias. We simply are not, and cannot be, all knowing and completely objective. Our understandings and views of the world are partial, and reflect the circumstances of our particular lives. This is where a discipline like science comes in. It doesn't purge us of bias. But it extends what we can see and understand, while constraining bias. That is where I would stake my claim, at any rate. The constant back-and-forth between ideas and research results hammers away at bias and, just as important, often reveals aspects of reality that surpass our original ideas and insights. When that has happened—and it has—that is the direction our research goes in. I would like to see my strongest convictions as arising from that kind of revelation, not from prior belief, and I hope you will get a view of that experience as you read along.

Arising this way, several general patterns of findings have persistently emerged in this research. Seeing these patterns, more than any ideas or hunches I began this research with, has convinced me of the importance of identity contingencies and identity threat in our lives.

The first pattern is that despite the strong sense we have of ourselves as autonomous individuals, evidence consistently shows that contingencies tied to our social identities do make a difference in shaping our lives, from the way we perform in certain situations to the careers and friends we choose. As the white world-class sprinter takes the starting blocks in the 100-meter dash at the Olympic trials, he is as autonomous an individual as the black sprinters next to him. And they all face precisely the same 100 meters of free and open track. Nonetheless, in order to do well in that situation, research suggests that he may have to surmount a pressure tied to his racial identity that the black sprinters don't face.

The second dimension of reality, long evident in our research, is that identity threats—and the damage they can do to our functioning—play an important role in some of society's most important social problems. These range from the racial, social class, and gender achievement gaps that persistently plague and distort our society to the equally persistent intergroup tensions that often trouble our social relations.

Third, also coming to light in this research is a general process—involving the allocation of mental resources and even a precise pattern of brain activation—by which these threats impair a broad range of human functioning. Something like a unifying understanding of how these threats have their effect is emerging.

Finally, a set of things we can do as individuals to reduce the impact of these threats in our own lives, as well as what we as a society can do to reduce their impact in important places like schools and workplaces, has come to light. There is truly inspirational news here: evidence that often small, feasible things done to reduce these threats in schools and classrooms can dramatically reduce the racial and gender achievement gaps that so discouragingly characterize our society.

These findings have convinced me of the importance of understanding identity threat to our personal progress, in areas of great concern like achievement and better group relations, and to societal progress, in achieving the identity-integrated civil life and equal opportunity that is a founding dream of this society. This book presents the journey that my colleagues and I have taken in getting to this conviction.

Let's begin the journey where it began—Ann Arbor, Michigan, 1987.

CHAPTER 2

A Mysterious Link Between Identity and Intellectual Performance

1.

In the spring of 1986, when I was a professor of psychology at the University of Washington in Seattle, the University of Michigan offered me a job with two parts. The first part was to be a social psychologist, just as I had been at the University of Washington. I was gratified: the University of Michigan had (and still has) one of the nation's leading graduate programs in social psychology. The second part was to direct an academic-support program for minority students. I was attracted to this too; an interest in the psychological issues surrounding the education of minority students had helped steer me into social psychology. But I worried. How would the "real-time" duties of running a student program affect my research? I visited the program twice to find out.

My second visit to Ann Arbor, toward the end of a steamy July, when the sidewalks radiated heat, proved decisive. I could see how big the program was. It served the advising, tutoring, and financial management needs of over 400 students, and it did so within a large bureaucracy, the kind that it takes to run a university of 36,000 students. I knew quickly on this second visit that I wouldn't take the job. I would have had to stop being a researcher, and I wasn't close to being ready for that. So I knew what to do. But I also knew, as I flew home, that something had changed for me, that seeing the program had caused a realignment of interests. What I'd seen, I felt, was a core American struggle: an institution trying to integrate itself, racially, ethnically, class-wise. The program staff and faculty had a mission. They were helping students from underrepresented backgrounds be effective on a demanding campus, one that, for example, had been racially integrated, to any meaningful degree, for only 20 or so years of its 170-year history. My research life, my intellectual life, I knew from this visit, would be headed in a different direction.

Two things, I believe, triggered the change. The first was a new vantage point on a familiar problem, the academic struggles of too many minority students on American college campuses. My Ann Arbor visit made me aware that I had a certain perspective on this problem, that I wasn't neutral. When it came to college student life, I was on the outside looking in, an observer. If asked to explain the academic difficulties of any students, I would, like most professors, have stressed what was in my observer's line of vision and in my psychologist's toolbox—the students themselves, their motivations, expectations, self-esteem, cultural orientation; the value they placed on education; their work habits; their academic skills and knowledge; their families' emphasis on school achievement; and so forth.

Some years ago, two social psychologists, Edward Jones and Richard Nisbett, argued that when it comes to explaining people's behavior—something like achievement problems, for example—there is a big difference between the "observer's perspective"—the perspective of a person observing the behavior—and the "actor's perspective"—the perspective of a person doing the behavior. As observers, Jones and Nisbett said, we're looking at the actor, the person doing the behavior we are trying to explain. Thus the actor dominates our literal and mental visual field, which makes the circumstances to which he is responding less visible to us. In the resulting picture in our minds, the actor sticks out like a sore thumb and the circumstances to which he is responding are obscured from view. Jones and Nisbett held that this picture causes a bias when we try to explain the actor's behavior. We emphasize the things we can see. We emphasize things about the actor—characteristics, traits, and so on—that seem like plausible explanations for her behavior. And we deemphasize, as causes of her behavior, the things we can't see very well, namely, the circumstances to which she is adapting. My second visit to Ann Arbor made me aware of what should have been obvious; I had become an observer of minority students and their achievement struggles. I arrived in Ann Arbor implicitly looking for what the students might be doing, or what characteristics they might have that held back their achievement.

But on the visit I talked to minority students themselves, the actors in the drama of their achievement struggles. They said nothing about expectations, motivation, the value their families placed on education—not even when I pointedly asked them about these things. They were proud to be students at such a strong university. Their families were proud of them. They had been successful in high school. If they brought low expectations with them, they didn't show them to me. They talked about the university environment. They talked about being a small social minority. They described needing a space where they weren't made so aware of being a minority. They worried that teaching assistants, fellow students, and even faculty might see their academic abilities as less than those of other students. They described how social life was organized by race, ethnicity, social class. They had few close friends across group lines. They felt that black styles, preferences, and interests were marginalized on campus, sometimes even stigmatized. They noted the small number of black or minority faculty. They could have been making excuses. I couldn't know. They seemed earnest, matter-of-fact, not accusatory. But they did seem worried that Michigan was not the right place for them.

The second striking thing I saw on this trip was a graph depicting student grades. It was my first glimpse of an important fact: that the academic troubles of black students at Michigan—and they were indeed having academic troubles—were not entirely due to weaker academic skills and motivations. After forming groups of Michigan graduates (for a period of several years) on the basis of the SAT score they had when they entered Michigan, the graph showed the average grades each of these groups got. Thus one could see the college grades for students who entered Michigan with SATs between 1000 and 1050, between 1050 and 1100, all the way up to those who entered with SATs between 1550 and 1600, then the top of the SAT scale. The graph showed a modest tendency for students with higher SATs to get higher grades. No surprise. The SAT is designed to predict college grades—even though, for this sample of students, the tendency for students with higher SATs to get higher college grades wasn't that strong.

What struck me was something else. To show how black students had done, the graph presented a separate line for black Michigan graduates during this same period. This line showed that black students with stronger entering SATs also graduated with slightly higher grades. Again, no surprise, except for one thing: the line for black students was consistently lower than the line for other students. At every level of entering SATs, even the highest level, black students got lower grades than other students. If we assume the SAT is a rough measure of preparation for college, this meant something dramatic: *that among students with comparable academic skills, as measured by the SAT, black students got less of a return on those skills in college than other students.* Something was suppressing the yield they got from their skills.

The Ann Arbor trip raised questions and provided some clues. There was hard evidence: the achievement problems of black students at Michigan weren't caused entirely by skill deficits. Something about the social and psychological aspects of their experience was likely involved. At the time, I had no idea what it was. There was softer evidence: the students themselves worried about whether or not they belonged, or ever could belong, at Michigan. Martin Luther King once worried that black students in integrated schools might not always be taught by people who "loved them." These students had the same concern. I wondered on that flight home whether these two pieces of evidence—about their grades and about their sense of belonging—had anything to do with each other.

2.

A year later Michigan offered me a professorship in psychology, a chance to pursue my research interests without administering a larger bureaucracy. I was excited. I knew that if I went, intriguing and important questions awaited.

Families can be gracious, and mine certainly was on this occasion. In the fall of 1987, despite the uprooting of two teenagers that it required, my family and I landed in Ann Arbor just in time for the new school year and Michigan football. Almost immediately, as if on signal, the graph showing black student underperformance at Michigan reappeared in my life. I was appointed to a universitywide committee on minority student retention and recruitment. And there again, in material handed out on the first day the committee met, was the graph showing the underperformance of black students, which was the chief rationale for this committee.

Richard Nisbett—another Michigan social psychologist, the same person who came up with the "actor-observer" difference—and I began talking about this underperformance. Nisbett is a great conversationalist, and not just idly so. He uses conversations to shape a scientific inquiry, to help him link up questions so that they have a narrative form. He starts in on a problem by trying to see how it works in real life. He interviews people. He surveys people over the phone. He snoops in archival records. He reads broadly. He "triangulates" on an understanding. Eventually he does formal experiments to test that understanding and to take the phenomenon further apart to see how it works. Inspired by this approach, I suppressed my normal tendency to proceed quickly to the laboratory.

I kept talking to students. I designed a seminar on the topic of underperformance. I remember that students in the seminar turned up a surprising fact. They stopped a number of black and white students as they crossed campus and asked them to complete a four- or five-page questionnaire. They wanted to find out how many close friends of a different race students had. The first page of the questionnaire asked students to list their six best friends, and the last page asked them to record their race. (This was so that a possible friend's race couldn't influence whether or not he or she was included on the list of close friends.) The

survey revealed that among their six closest friends, neither white
nor black students averaged even one friend from the other racial
group. Blacks, for example, averaged only two-thirds of a white
friend among their top six friends. As students had been telling
me, their social networks were organized by race.

I continued to look at grade records. I wanted to see how common black student underperformance was across the curriculum.
Sadly, it was everywhere, from English to math to psychology.
As some comfort to the University of Michigan, my reading soon
revealed that black student underperformance was a national phenomenon. It happened throughout the education system, in college
classes, in medical schools, in law schools, in business schools, and
often in K through 12 schooling. It was so common and predict-
able as to be nearly lawful. People who made tests had long known
about this phenomenon. They also knew that it happens to more
groups than just blacks. It happens to Latinos, Native Americans,
and to women in advanced college math classes, law schools, medical schools, and business schools.

This is, of course, an unhappy fact. And standing at the ready
I found many explanations, largely from the observer's perspective:
that these students lack the motivation or cultural knowledge or
skills to succeed at more difficult coursework where underperformance tends to occur, or that they somehow self-destruct because
of low self-expectations or low self-esteem picked up from the
broader culture, or even from their own families and communities.
These accounts weren't implausible, if not entirely handsome. I had
to keep them on the table of possibilities. But I had doubts. Could
they fully explain the occurrence of underperformance in so many
groups, at so many levels and types of schooling?

Nor could I shake a suspicion that, to a larger extent than I and
others had realized, underperformance had something to do with
what underperforming groups were experiencing in school. Some-

thing was causing their strengths to let them down consistently—even the strongest among them. Something in the air on campus seemed part of their problems.

3.

A few years later I was invited to give a talk on my research at a small, distinguished liberal arts college in the Northeast. The school also took the occasion to consult me about the progress of their minority students, which, in the early 1990s, meant largely black students. This would turn out to be something I did often in the years to come. Invariably, I learned a lot on these trips. They always edified, showing me things about the problems I was working on that I hadn't understood before.

This early trip was especially interesting. I talked to black student groups and to faculty and administrators in rapid succession—a dramatic display of different perspectives.

The faculty and administrators worried about the problems of black students: lower grade performance, greater likelihood of dropping out, a greater tendency to downgrade their professional ambitions as their schooling went on, a tendency to avoid quantitatively based fields, less social integration into campus life, significantly segregated friendship networks, and so on. Their list was nearly identical to the list drawn up by the Michigan recruitment and retention committee.

We talked in a small conference room paneled in light maple. One entire wall was floor-to-ceiling windows that brought in slants of early spring light and the sight of patchy snow in the woods outside. The atmosphere was friendly, even warm, but also serious, careful—conducive to a trusting conversation among the adults. These were busy people. The problems of black students on this privileged campus weren't their only concerns. They wanted their school to work well, however, and to work well for everyone.

They used primarily "observer" theories to understand these problems. Were they admitting the right students? Should they weigh academic skills even more heavily in admissions? Was family background critical? They hadn't heard of the underperformance phenomenon. They weren't sure about its implication that the problems of these students weren't entirely academic. I also felt a presence in the room during the faculty and administrator meetings; it was as if a flame burned in the corner. The flame was the possibility that, inadvertently, they might do something or condone something that could be seen as racist. It was a searing flame. They didn't want to get close to it. They wanted me to talk. Did I have any ideas?

The black students, for their part, were distressed. I met them in a long, narrow, low-ceilinged room on the first floor of a campus house that had been converted to student service offices and meeting rooms. Students crowded in for the session, probably seventy-five or so in number, a fair portion of their population on this small campus. They wanted me to talk too, but mainly they wanted to talk. They wanted to describe their experience at the college, the stress they felt. They said that too much of the time they felt that they didn't belong. They said they were unhappy a lot of the time. They often went home on weekends. Did I have any ideas?

Sometimes black students said the school had racist elements. They fanned the flame. They would cite an incident with a teaching assistant, a comment by a professor or fellow student. But as the day went on and I got to look over their shoulders more—take the "actor's" perspective—it seemed to me that they were affected more by the ways campus life was racially organized than by the racism of particular people.

There was, for example, their sense of marginalization. They were a small minority on campus. Campus culture—its ideas of who and what were "cool," its prevailing values, social norms, preferences, modes of dress, images of beauty, musical preferences, modes of religious expression, and the like—was dominated by whites, the most numerous group on campus and the group most historically identified with the school. Against this backdrop, black students worried about belonging, about whether they could find a valued place in campus life. Could they be valued for who they were in this setting? Would they be seen as socially desirable? Numbers played a big role in this sense of marginalization. The cultural domination of whites followed from their numbers.

Friendships and social life were also significantly organized by race. Black students were clearly party to this, even as they seemed to sense its costs. Over 85 percent of Americans, for example, get their jobs through acquaintance contacts. Racially homogeneous friendship networks can segregate people out of important networks, and thus out of important opportunities. They also noted the small number of black faculty and administrators. Was this irrelevant? Did it say something about the possibility of their belonging on this campus?

The sociologist William Julius Wilson has explained the creation and maintenance of large African American ghettos in northern cities as due to a "concentration" of factors, such as the long period of migration of blacks from the South to the North, inadequate and poorly funded public schools, the movement of jobs outside of the cities and to foreign countries, job discrimination, and geographic and social isolation. These things combine, in the philosopher Charles Mills's term, to "downwardly constitute" people living in ghettos, to so disadvantage them as to make them less effective agents in their own behalf.

This tidy, well-off college was no racial ghetto. And the factors that "downwardly constitute" black students there were less commonly understood than factors like distance from jobs or discrimination. But listening to these students, it seemed that a "concentration of factors" provided a better way to understand what might be causing their underperformance. The major standing explanations seemed incomplete. Underperformance didn't seem to be fully explained by racism on the part of teachers and fellow students. The instances of possible racism that black students described weren't nearly as lawful and widespread as their underperformance. Nor did it seem to be caused simply by motivational or cultural deficits that black students brought with them. These students were the academic vanguard of their group, for the most part selected against the highest academic standards. Rather, a concentration of factors seemed to be involved: a concentration of racialized aspects of campus life—racial marginalization, racial segregation of social and academic networks, group underrepresentation in important campus roles, even a racial organization of curriculum choices, all reflecting, to some degree, the racial organization of the larger society.

This seemed like a reasonable hunch. Still, as I said, these weren't "hard" factors like unemployment and unequal school financing. They were dimensions of social organization. How bad could they be? Could they really be powerful enough to interfere with grade performance of black students, especially of black students very likely reared with the value of trying "twice as hard" in the face of racial adversity?

4.

On April 4, 1968, Martin Luther King Jr. was assassinated. On the next day, a third-grade teacher in Iowa named Jane Elliott was looking for a way to show her class the importance of Dr. King's life and work. She lived in Riceville, Iowa, a small farming community with a population so homogeneous that many of her students had never seen an African American. To show them the experience of being discriminated against, she divided her class into brown-eyed and blue-eyed students. On the first day, she discriminated against the brown-eyed students. She put felt collars around their necks to identify them. She said that blue-eyed students were smarter, cleaner, and better behaved than brown-eyed students. She gave blue-eyed students seats in the front of the classroom and first dibs on playground equipment during recess. She encouraged the blue-eyed students not to associate with the brown-eyed students, in class or on the playground. She gave blue-eyed students first access to lessons and materials used in the lessons. The entire exercise was eventually reenacted and made into an ABC News documentary entitled "The Eye of the Storm."

Even in the reenactment, the emotion on the faces of the brown-eyed students on that first day was upsetting. You knew this exercise wouldn't be repeated much. The students were humiliated; they huddled together on the playground, coat collars turned up to hide their faces from the documentary's camera. They said almost nothing in class and barely spoke all day. The blue-eyed students, meanwhile, were relaxed, happy, unself-conscious participants in class.

On the second day Ms. Elliott turned the tables. She put the felt collars around the necks of the blue-eyed students and treated them the same way she'd treated the brown-eyed students the day before. The blue-eyed students now lost the energy they'd had the day before and behaved the way the brown-eyed students had on that day, huddled and downcast. The brown-eyed students, for their part, were once again eager learners.

Tucked away in this documentary are several scenes showing a fascinating intellectual implication of Ms. Elliott's experiment. These are the scenes in which she gives arithmetic and spelling lessons to small groups of students. They show how poorly the stigmatized students did. They barely paid attention. They receded to the back of even these small groups. They spoke only if spoken to. They didn't remember the instructions. They were slow to respond. They got a lot of answers wrong. But on the day they were not stigmatized, these same students responded like the exuberant, cognitively adept children they apparently were. The environment, and their status in it, seemed to be an actual component of their ability.

Ms. Elliott deliberately set out to downwardly constitute her students, temporarily. She was making a point. The college I visited was not making a point. It did not purposely set out to do things that would downwardly constitute black students. Quite the contrary. It saw itself as committed to their inclusion. The school was bewildered by the problems that followed that inclusion. But after I thought about group underperformance for a number of years, and talked to countless students along the way, two things occurred to me. First, like many institutions of higher education in the United States, this school had inherited a social organization from the larger society and from its own history that might well place black students under downwardly constituting pressures— powerful pressures not well understood within the traditional frameworks of prejudice and racism, on the one hand, or student deficits, on the other. Second, these downwardly constituting pressures might have the power to interfere directly and indirectly with *intellectual* performance. That is, they might have the power to cause underperformance.

5.

By this time, I was working with a University of Michigan graduate student named Steven Spencer (now a distinguished professor at the University of Waterloo). Steve is a high-energy, enthusiastic person. He grew up on a Michigan farm. He knows how to throw himself into things. He loves to talk psychology. He is quick and incisive. We had been working on the question of how people maintain a perception of personal adequacy in the face of information that could threaten that perception. The effort to do this, we theorized, is a major driver of mental life, causing us to reexamine our beliefs and assumptions, to reintegrate understandings, sometimes even to prod growth. Our approach to understanding these questions had earlier been pulled together in a theory of self-affirmation. That theory and an unrelated, but equally interesting theory of how the pharmacological and psychological effects of alcohol could foster alcohol addiction, had been the foci of my research at the University of Washington. These were captivating problems, fun to work on. Steve and I, along with Robert Josephs (another graduate student at the time, now a distinguished professor at the University of Texas), were making great progress in both areas.

But for some reason, at this new university, it was the problem of group underperformance that had begun to preoccupy me. I kibitzed and kibitzed about it, and eventually, as I had hoped, Steve began to pick up this preoccupation too.

Despite the image of science as a formal and prescribed affair, scientific inquiries have choice points, places where the investigator has to decide what to do next without much formal guidance. Intuition and best guesses come into play. We needed a better look at what caused underperformance, and my best hunch was that it was stigmatization, the downward constitution that some groups might experience in a school environment. Of course, underperformance could just as well come from something about the group itself. I favored the stigmatization idea. I confess that I liked it better than the idea that underperformance was rooted in some biological difference between groups—to me a discouraging and potentially dehumanizing idea. But there was also the fact that scholastic underperformance happened in several groups—blacks, Latinos, Native Americans, women in math classes. Could there be something biological about all of these groups that caused them to underperform? Possibly, but I could also imagine that these groups shared an experience of stigmatization—different in form, of course, but nonetheless a group-based stigmatization in precisely those areas where they underperformed. A reasonable inference, but only an inference. I knew it was time to test this idea.

To do this, Steve and I needed a situation like Jane Elliott's classroom. We had to compare a group's intellectual performance when its members were stigmatized with their intellectual performance when they were not stigmatized—like comparing the blue-eyed students' performance on the day they wore collars and were seated in the back of the classroom with their performance on the day they wore no collars and were seated up front. If the group members underperformed when they were stigmatized, but not when they were not stigmatized, we'd have evidence that stigmatization alone—a devalued social status—had the capacity to impair intellectual performance.

It soon occurred to us that a natural experiment of precisely this sort might be going on in our own backyard, the college classroom, specifically in the different experiences of women in math-oriented versus humanities-oriented classes. Considerable research shows that in math classes, especially at the college level and especially in more advanced classes, women report feeling what the sociologists Nancy Hewitt and Elaine Seymour called a "chilly climate." That is, they feel that their abilities are under suspicion, that feminine characteristics discredit their seriousness, that they have to prove themselves constantly, that their career commitment is questioned, and so on. Yet in English classes, and in humanities classes more generally, women report fewer such pressures, even in advanced coursework.

Steve and I weren't focused on the question of why these differences exist. This book returns to that question at various points. At the time, though, he and I were focused on a simpler idea: the natural experiment this situation would allow.

We could compare how much women underperformed in advanced math classes, where they reported feeling more stigmatization from a "chilly climate," with how much they underperformed in advanced English classes, where they reported feeling considerably less stigmatization of their abilities. The experiment was just that simple. If stigmatization can impair intellectual performance, as Steve and I were guessing, then women in advanced math classes should underperform more than women in advanced English classes. That is, the gap between women's and men's grades should be greater in advanced math classes than in advanced English classes.

The data we could assemble were less than perfect. (It is important to stress that once the data were assembled, the names of all students were replaced with identification numbers to protect their anonymity.) There were very few women in advanced math classes. Some students had to be dropped because we couldn't retrieve SAT scores for them and, thus, couldn't put them into an SAT score grouping.

Still, a pattern that mirrored the scenes in Jane Elliott's classroom emerged. Women tended to underperform in advanced math classes, where evidence suggests they feel the collar of gender stigma, but not in advanced English classes, where evidence suggests the collar is less felt.

Seeing underperformance, especially among such talented and motivated people in real-life classrooms, is disheartening. But this time, at least, the pattern of when it happened and when it didn't happen told us something about its causes. It encouraged our thinking about stigma and intellectual performance.

Nonetheless, the quality of the data was worrisome, and we knew that our results could be explained in other ways than by our theory. Perhaps the men in the English classes were less interested than the men in the math classes. Maybe that's why they didn't outperform the women in those classes. Or maybe the work in the English classes was just easier than the work in the math classes, enabling all students to get higher grades. In the real world of college classes, many factors could be at play.

We needed a more precise test of whether or not stigma impaired intellectual performance. We also knew that if the effect was real and we could reliably produce it—if we could "bottle" this effect in the laboratory, so to speak—we could use the laboratory procedure to answer other important questions: What factors worsened this effect? What exactly does stigmatization do to people that impairs their intellectual functioning? Are some kinds of people more susceptible to this effect than others? Does it happen for all stigmatized groups or just some? Does it happen for other kinds of performance, in addition to intellectual performance? Does it happen for low-stakes performances or just high-stakes performances? And, most important, what can be done to eliminate it?

Our approach was to reproduce our math and English study in the laboratory. We set up a very simple situation. First, we recruited men and women students at the University of Michigan, largely freshmen and sophomores, who were good at math—they had quantitative SAT scores in the top 15 percent of their entering class, had gotten at least a B in two calculus classes, and indicated that math was important to their personal and professional goals. This gave us a group of men and women students who were essentially equal and strong in math skills and in commitment to math. We then brought them into the laboratory one at a time and gave them a very difficult intellectual test alone in a room.

That was the core of the experiment. But, of course, we wanted half of these participants to take the test under stigmatizing or potentially stigmatizing conditions and the other half to take the test under nonstigmatizing conditions.

Again, we mimicked our field study. We varied the topic of the test, math versus English. Half of the participants took a math test, a thirty-minute section of the GRE (Graduate Record Examination) in math; the other half took an English test, a thirty-minute section of the GRE in English literature, a heavily knowledge-based test. (These sections were taken not from the general quantitative or verbal portion of the GRE but from the more difficult GRE subject tests in math and English.)

We reasoned as follows: On the basis of negative stereotypes of women's math ability, simply taking a difficult math test puts a woman at risk of stigmatization, of being seen as limited at math *because she is a woman*. Frustration on such a test inherently reinforces this worry.

By contrast, no stereotype says men *as a group* lack math ability. They might lack it as individuals. Frustration on the test could reflect that. But it wouldn't mean that they lacked math ability because they were men.

And for the same reason, there should be no threat of group stigmatization for either men or women taking the English literature test. The ability of neither group is strongly stigmatized in this area, although we did wonder whether men might feel some threat of group stigmatization on the literature test.

We had, then, a laboratory facsimile of our real-life field study. If having the collar on—being at risk of group stigmatization—was enough to interfere with intellectual performance, then the women should underperform in relation to the men on the math test, where they were subject to stigmatization, but not on the English literature test, where neither group was subject to stigmatization. And, lo and behold, that's exactly what happened.

We were encouraged. Not because we'd proved anything— there was at least one especially plausible alternative explanation that I will describe just ahead. But now we had laboratory procedures that reproduced what we'd seen in the real world. And they were relatively safe. We didn't have to put participants through anything they didn't go through all of the time; it was just test taking. Moreover, by explaining the experiment to them after it was over—"debriefing" them—we might help them better cope with these pressures in their own lives. We had a safe version of Jane Elliott's classroom, a place where the possible effect of stigmatization on intellectual performance could be looked at up close, where we could learn how it happened and, possibly, how to reduce it.

6.

We believed it was the pressure not to confirm a stigmatizing view of oneself that made women underperform in this experiment. But there was a compelling, if disturbing, alternative possibility that had been brought gingerly to our attention: perhaps women's lower performance reflected a lesser biological capacity for math that manifests itself on difficult math.

In the early 1980s, two psychologists, Camilla Benbow and Julian Stanley, conducted several large studies of sex differences in math performance that were reported in the prestigious journal *Science*. Interestingly, the design of their study was not unlike the design of our study. They, too, selected students who were very good at math. Theirs were eighth-grade boys and girls who had had essentially the same coursework in math up to that point, and who had scored in the top 3 percent of test takers on the standardized math exam given to eighth-graders at their schools. They then gave students a math test that was very difficult for eighth-graders, the math section of the SAT. Their results looked like ours. The girls underperformed in relation to the boys. And because the boys and girls in this study had been so carefully selected for having equal math skills and equal exposure to math instruction up to that point, Benbow and Stanley were pushed to a difficult conclusion: perhaps the lower performance of girls in their study reflected a lesser biological capacity for math among women that reveals itself when the math was difficult.

Our society is fascinated by genetic explanations of everything from alcoholism and hyperactivity to happiness. The idea that genetics underlies the sex difference in math performance—just like the racial differences in athletic performance that I mentioned earlier—seems destined to fascinate us. For example, in January of 2005, in a speech given at the Massachusetts Institute of Technology (MIT) to kick off a conference on women's presence in science, the then president of Harvard University, Larry Summers, said,

> There are three broad hypotheses about the sources of the very substantial disparities that this conference's papers document and have been documented before with respect to women in high-end scientific professions. One is what I would call the high-powered job hypothesis. The second is what I would call *the differential availability of aptitude at the high end*, and the third is what I would call different socialization and patterns of dis-

crimination in a search. And in my view their importance ranks in exactly the order I have just described.

In the middle of his speech, Nancy Hopkins, a distinguished biologist from MIT, walked out. Soon the conference was in turmoil—largely in argument over the intended meaning of Summers's "second hypothesis." Within hours the media had begun to cover the turmoil, interviewing conferees as witnesses to Summers's remarks. Within days op-ed pages, television and radio talk shows, and media pundits had all focused attention on his remarks and on the arguments of his supporters and detractors. Soon some people called on Summers to resign. Protests at Harvard University intensified in the weeks and months that followed the conference. On March 15 of that year, the members of the Faculty of Arts and Sciences at Harvard voted 218 to 185 that they no longer had confidence in Summers as president of Harvard University. He weathered this vote, supported by the Harvard Corporation, the body of trustees that governs Harvard. But a year later, to forestall another faculty vote of no confidence, Summers resigned. By this time, other issues in his presidency had surfaced. The debate over his leadership had broadened. But few would argue that the unraveling of the Summers's presidency began with what he thought was a passing reference to his "second hypothesis"—that sex differences in math and science achievement were substantially rooted in sex differences in a genetically based capacity for math.

Steve Spencer and I weren't especially interested in the genetic explanation of sex differences in math. Our idea was that stigma had more to do with these differences than people commonly thought. But we knew, long before the Summers episode, that the genetic question carried huge cultural weight. Also, it stood as a possible alternative explanation for our experimental findings. We had to address it.

This was no small moment in our nascent research program. We'd gotten to a point where two plausible, but very different, ideas could explain our simple finding that, after we had carefully selected women and men who had strong and equal math skills, the women did worse on a difficult math test we gave them than the men—that is, classic underperformance. Our explanation was that frustration during a difficult math test made women worry about confirming, or being seen to confirm, the societal view about women's poor math ability, and that this worry, in turn, interfered with their performance. This is how we saw the "collar" of stigma interfering with math.

The other explanation was simply that women's underperformance was caused by something about women, a psychological vulnerability, or something perhaps akin to Summers's "second hypothesis."

We needed an experiment that could tell us which of the two was the better account of our findings. This is both a fun and a tense part of science: pitting two ideas against each other in an empirical test. If you come up with a good empirical test, you hope to get a clear answer. In this case, a clear answer would have implications. It would tell us whether our earlier experiments had found a truly undiscovered influence on women's math performance—a stigma-related contingency of gender identity in the United States—or whether they merely point to a long-surmised limitation in women's math capacity that manifests itself on difficult math. It would be an experiment with real stakes.

But what would that experiment be?

In trying to figure that out, we realized something else about our explanation. For motivated women taking a difficult math test, we were arguing that the pressure not to confirm the stereotype was part of their *normal* experience in taking difficult math tests. All it took for them to feel this pressure was frustration, inevitable on a difficult math test. Frustration would make the cultural stereotype come to mind and be seen as relevant to them personally. This meant that nothing extra was needed to impose this pressure. Just give math-motivated women a hard math test and they'd feel it automatically—in our laboratory, and presumably, in real life. Thus the challenge in setting up a good experiment was not that of finding something extra to real life that would put this pressure on women during a math test. The challenge was to find something extra to real life that would lower the pressure women normally feel during such tests, that would somehow remove the "collar" of stigma during difficult math tests.

If lowering this pressure improved women's test performance, then we'd know that it was this pressure that undermined their performance in our earlier experiments.

But how to lower this pressure?

We first thought of trying to persuade them that the negative stereotype about women and math was false. If they didn't believe the stereotype, perhaps they wouldn't worry about confirming it. But then we realized that, even if we could convince them of this, it was doubtful we could convince them that other people didn't believe the stereotype, broadly held as it is. And if we couldn't convince them of that, they could still worry that their test performance would cause other people—the experimenter perhaps—to see them stereotypically.

We stewed, feet on our desks; then we had a simple idea. We'd present the test in a way that made the cultural stereotype about women's math ability irrelevant to their performance. We'd say something like this: "You may have heard that women don't do as well as men on difficult standardized math tests, but that's not true for the *particular* standardized math test; on this *particular* test, women always do as well as men." (This is a close rendition of what was actually said in the real experiment.)

It was a simple instruction. But presenting the test this way changed the meaning of any frustration women experienced. It made it not a sign of anything about being a woman, because this "particular test" couldn't measure anything about being a woman, or about gender in general, for that matter. They were now in the same boat as men taking this test. Their frustration could confirm that they weren't good at math as individuals, but it couldn't confirm that they weren't good at math because they were women.

A change of instruction and a contingency of their gender identity that normally haunted them during difficult math would be gone.

So we had a plan. We would do the experiment as before. We would recruit strong women and men math students at Michigan. We would give them all a difficult math test alone in a room. And for the group in which we didn't want the women to experience the risk of stigma, we'd present the test as not showing gender differences.

This would put in place all of the elements we needed to pit the two big ideas against each other in an empirical test. If women for whom stigma pressure was lowered performed as well as equally skilled men in this experiment, we'd know that stigma pressure had worsened their performance in the earlier studies. We'd know that this pressure could have a big effect on women's math performance. But if lowering this pressure had no effect on women's test performance—if the women still performed worse than equally-skilled men—then we'd know that this pressure wasn't a factor in our earlier findings, that something else was. Perhaps something about how women are socialized, or perhaps . . . Summers's "second hypothesis."

At this point in our research, Steve and I weren't especially focused on larger implications. But for this experiment we knew the stakes were high. We were excited but tense.

And the results were dramatic. They gave us a clear answer. Among participants who were told the test did show gender differences, where the women could still feel the threat of stigma confirmation, women did worse than equally skilled men, just as in the earlier experiment. But among participants who were told the test *did not* show gender differences, where the women were free of confirming anything about being a woman, *woman performed at the same high level as equally skilled men. Their underperformance was gone.*[*]

It is no exaggeration to say that these findings changed the course of our research lives. It gave us the first empirical signal that the stigma pressure we had been theorizing about was actually powerful enough to affect the ordinary experience of women doing math, especially math at the limits of their skills, where frustration is inevitable. It simultaneously told us that women's underperformance in math, where it happened, might be more fixable than people thought. Removing the threat of stereotype confirmation that normally hangs over the heads of women doing difficult math, dramatically improved their performance—the way removing the collar from Jane Elliott's students improved their performance.

By no means did we have a complete explanation of these findings. This book will have a lot more to tell about that. Also, we had to be careful about generalizing our findings. They did not mean, for example, that removing stigma threat would eliminate all sex differences in math performance. Most observed sex differ-

---

[*]The experience closest to real life in this experiment was that of women in the group that was led to believe that the math test showed gender differences. In this experiment, we explicitly stated this to participants in this group. In later research that would prove unnecessary. Strong women math students underperformed on tests like this one without being reminded that it showed gender differences. They simply assumed it.

ences in math performance are not between samples of men and women selected for being similar in math skills and motivation, as they were in our experiments. They are between samples of men and women who may differ in skills and motivation, because of differential exposure to math curriculum, different interest in math, different exposure to stigma threat over a lifetime, and so on. Taking off the collar of stigma threat on one occasion might well reduce these differences on that occasion, but not necessarily eliminate them altogether.

Still, the findings clearly told Steve and me that we had an important phenomenon to figure out, one that might be playing an especially unfortunate role in women's progress in math-related fields.

Research has shown that the further women go in mathematics, the harder it is for them to persist. Many factors contribute to this—the sex roles women are socialized into, perhaps discrimination against women in math, perhaps low expectations about their abilities. Steve and I felt we'd found another possibility: the threat of confirming, or being seen to confirm, society's darker suspicions about their math ability, a threat that reoccurs at precisely the worst point in their progression from stage to stage in math achievement—that next frontier of their skills.

It was this finding that changed our research lives, and that gave us marching orders.

But we had to admit that our idea was unusual. The crumbs leading to it were consistent: my student interviews, the data showing the underperformance phenomenon, and now our experiments with women in math. Still, it was an unusual idea—suggesting, as it did, that stereotypes of groups (for example, stereotypes about women's math ability) could cause enough disruption to interfere with the math performance of strong women math students on a standardized test, and possibly with their persistence in math altogether.

It was also unusual because it suggested this could happen without bad intentions, without the agency of prejudiced people, for example. Our test takers were alone in a room. They had no reason to believe that the experiment was run by people biased against women. What they did know, of course, was the culture of this society. They knew how people in this culture tend to see math ability, as something men have more of than women. They knew their performance could confirm that view. And for these women invested in math, this conjunction of thoughts was upsetting and distracting enough to interfere with their performance.

Nor was our idea in general use. It didn't appear on the list of reasons in the research literature as to why few women reach elite levels of math and science. We presented developing versions of the idea at conferences. People liked the finding that women's math performance could be dramatically improved by removing the risk of confirming the negative view of women's math ability. But they had a difficult time keeping our explanation in mind as a distinct idea. They'd boil it down to something else. They'd say, "Aren't you just saying that women have lower *expectations* for their math performance, and that when they encounter difficult math they just *self-fulfill* those low expectations?" We'd thought about this point. But it didn't explain our results. The women in our experiments were selected for having strong expectations. They had always been good at math, and they performed well when told the test couldn't detect gender differences. If difficult math triggered low expectations that, in self-fulfillment, caused women to underperform, then these women, too, should have underperformed. They didn't.

We thought we had something distinct. Still, we recognized that we knew more about what it wasn't than about what it was.

There were many questions. How did this pressure impair performance? Through memory impairment? Extra cognitive load? Physiological impairment? Did it affect only people who cared about the performance? Did it affect only women in relation to math, or did it also affect other groups and other types of performance? Could it be overcome with more effort, or did that effort just make matters worse? Were there things that schools and teachers could do to relieve these pressures? Were there things that individuals could do to relieve them?

Important questions—all of which, in time, would be researched, and many of which would be answered. But at the time, in the context of a different collaboration, my curiosity turned back to the question of minority student achievement. Could the same process that affected women math students be a factor in the underperformance of minority students?

CHAPTER 3

Stereotype Threat Comes to Light, and in More than One Group

1.

In 1978, when I lived in Seattle, the Seattle Supersonics came within one game of winning the NBA championship. The next year, they won. Their ascent to glory followed a long period of mediocrity. The 1978 season, in fact, began in mediocrity, 5 wins and 17 losses during the opening weeks of the season. Then the Sonics' front office fired the coach and hired a new one—a young Lenny Wilkens, who had been a player-coach with the team several years earlier. No player changes, just Wilkens. Instantly the team began to win, 42 season victories and only 18 losses under Wilkens. The regular season ended with a 47–35 record before the Sonics lost the NBA title by just 6 points in the final seconds of the seventh game of the championship series. A single personnel change—the addition of Wilkens—and the pieces of the team came together. What's interesting here is how the team was written about before and after its turnaround. Before the turnaround, the local sportswriters described player characteristics in the worst terms. The point guard could pass okay, but couldn't drive to the basket. The strong forward shot from too far out and missed easy rebounds under the basket. The center had too little mobility and couldn't get midrange shots. The sportswriters were observers. To make sense of things, they used what was in their line of vision—the players and their characteristics. And they had losses to explain. Sensibly, they stressed negative player deficiencies.

With a coaching change, the Sonics changed. Now the sportswriters had to explain winning, not losing. Their player characterizations changed. They valorized the same players they had derided a month earlier. The players' weaknesses became their strengths. The point guard's poor driving ability became a testament to his brilliance as a floor general; the strong forward's lack of rebounding was a minor cost of his beautiful outside shot; and the center's immobility made him a rock of stability under the basket. By the time the team reached the finals, the sportswriters saw genius in every position.

Explanations of underachievement by minority and women students are under the same constraints as explanations of the early 1978 Sonics. Almost invariably, they take an observer's perspective, and they are trying to explain poor performance, not success. Under these constraints, student deficiencies make sense as causes of these troubles, just as player deficiencies made sense as causes of the troubles of the early 1978 Sonics. There was then, like a specter hanging over our research, a long-standing tradition of how to explain the psychology of poor achievement among disadvantaged minorities and women.

2.

In his book *Contempt and Pity*, the intellectual historian Daryl Scott describes this social science tradition with a focus on the experience of African Americans. Like the sportswriters, social science observers have been trying to explain poor outcomes—economic, social, educational, medical—experienced by blacks throughout the twentieth century. Like the sportswriters, Scott argues, they have tended to focus on deficiencies, one of which dominates all others—what he calls "psychic damage."

It will be a familiar idea. Gordon Allport, the great mid-twentieth-century social psychologist, put it succinctly: "One's reputation, whether false or true, cannot be hammered, hammered, hammered, into one's head without doing something to one's character" (p. 142). The psyche of individual blacks gets damaged, the idea goes, by bad images of the group projected in society—images of blacks as aggressive, as less intelligent, and so on. Repeated exposure to these images causes these images to be "internalized," implicitly accepted as true of the group and, tragically, also perhaps of one's self. This internalization damages "character" by causing low self-esteem, low expectations, low motivation, self-doubt, and the like. And in turn, this damage contributes to a host of bad things, such as high unemployment, poor marriage success, low educational achievement, and criminality.

The idea, as Scott notes, is more than just a scientific idea. It's conventional wisdom, a virtual stereotype of what causes members of negatively regarded groups to fail. So if something causes black and women college students to perform less well than you'd expect from their skills, it must be—the idea goes—these psychic deficiencies, deficiencies of confidence and expectation, self-sabotaging deficiencies. This explanation followed logically from an observer's perspective, and it was supported by the weight of tradition. It pressed hard on my thinking as I thought about what to do next.

3.

Eventually the Seattle sportswriters broke set in 1978. They saw the Sonics for what they were. This wasn't due to their perceptiveness. The Sonics started to win with the same players. That made it clear. Player deficiencies couldn't have been the sole cause of the team's losing. The sportswriters, of course, hadn't been all wrong. The players had deficiencies, which surely contributed to their losing. But winning showed that these deficiencies weren't the sole cause. Something else was involved, something that Wilkens had figured out.

Like that of the Seattle sportswriters when the Sonics began to win, my own observer's perspective on the achievement of minority and women college students had been consistently unsettled by facts. It wasn't that these students had no deficiencies. Education is not equal in this society, in either access or quality. Socioeconomic disadvantage, segregating social practices, and restrictive cultural orientations have all dampened the educational opportunities of some groups more than others, historically and in ongoing ways. These differences might well yield corresponding group deficiencies in skill—enough to affect a group's college achievement, and enough for observers to point to. Still, the facts in my path consistently pointed away from these deficiencies as the sole cause.

And perhaps foremost among these facts was the type of students who participated in our research. They weren't underskilled, poorly motivated students from bad educational backgrounds. By any normal standard, they had no significant psychological or skill deficits. They were among the nation's top college students, admitted to one of its most selective universities. Also, I had seen underperformance among stronger as well as weaker students in Michigan's classrooms, and it clearly happened in most college classrooms, as the larger research literature revealed. The facts were stacking up against the deficiency idea as an adequate account of what I had seen and of what our experiments were showing.

But before getting too concerned about this, I knew I had to answer a more fundamental question first. I needed to know whether the effect of stigma pressure that Steve and I had observed in our experiments with women and math would generalize to other groups. Would this pressure affect the performance of other groups whose intellectual abilities were negatively viewed in the larger society? Would it affect the performance of, say, African Americans on a difficult standardized test—the group whose academic troubles hand launched this research?

4.

At about this time, in 1991, I moved again, from the University of Michigan in Ann Arbor to Stanford University—a move back to the family's beloved West Coast. Joining me was another wonderful collaborator, a freshly minted Ph.D. from Princeton University named Joshua Aronson (now an eminent professor at New York University). Josh had signed on as a postdoctoral student to research issues related to self-affirmation theory, which I mentioned my students and I had developed some years earlier. He had just completed an insightful dissertation on the topic. He has an intuitive feel for social psychology and for how to do experiments. But, like Steve earlier, Josh found himself working with a preoccupied professor, someone immersed in issues of underperformance, women in math, the possible effects of stigma on intellectual performance and persistence. These were the puzzles on the table. And Josh, intrigued by them and full of ideas, joined in trying to move the pieces around, trying to find a solution. I felt lucky. A shared puzzle gets solved much faster.

We considered the facts in front of us: the underperformance phenomenon, my interviews with women and black students, and the results of the Michigan experiments I had done with Steve. We lined up our questions. Of first importance was the generalization question: Would the effect of stigma pressure that Steve and I had observed with women and math generalize to another group whose intellectual abilities where not well regarded, such as African Americans, the group whose academic troubles had launched this research? If it did, we'd have good reason to believe that the effect of stigma pressure on intellectual functioning was a general phenomenon—that it could happen to members of any group some or all of whose intellectual abilities were viewed negatively in the larger society. If it didn't, we'd have to reconsider the possibility that women had some special vulnerability to this pressure.

A second question was whether an effect of stigma pressure, if it happened for black students, would happen for strong black students, as it had for strong women math students in the experiments with Steve. There was reason to wonder. In fact, reviewers of the grant proposal I had submitted to get funding for this research doubted this possibility altogether. They found it hard to believe that stigma pressure of the sort we had described could seriously disrupt the intellectual performance of strong, motivated black students at the nation's most prestigious universities. These students, they reasoned, would just be too strong or too motivated to be knocked off their game by such a pressure. We could see their point. It was, after all, less our intuition than our facts that had led us to this possibility. So we knew our challenge had two parts: first, to test whether the effects that Steve and I had gotten with women math students would also happen for black students

and, second, to test whether, if they happened, they would happen
with strong black students. It turned out that we were in precisely
the right place to test these questions: Stanford University, one of
the nation's most selective universities.

In no time we had an experiment. We invited black and white
Stanford students, predominantly sophomores, into our laboratory
one at a time and gave them a very difficult test of verbal reasoning
made up of items from the verbal section of the Advanced Graduate Record Examination. It was a difficult test for students at this
stage; student samples similar to those in our experiment had
gotten only 30 percent of the items correct in pretest administra-
tions of the test. It would cause frustration. As for women taking
a difficult math test, we assumed, this frustration would worry our
black participants, signaling as it might that they could be confirming the stereotype of their group's lesser intellectual ability. We
administered the test as it is administered in real life, nothing out
of the ordinary, and assumed that the frustration it caused would
be enough to make black students feel this threat.

White students wouldn't like frustration either. But they
wouldn't worry that it was confirming anything about their group,
since there is no broadly held negative stereotype in this society
about whites' having lower intelligence.

What happened is what was expected: white students did a lot
better on this difficult test than black students. They got, on average, four more items correct on this thirty-item, half-hour section
of the GRE—a large difference that, if sustained over the whole
GRE exam, would be very substantial.[*] As Steve and I had cap-

---

[*] It is important to stress that we used standard statistical procedures to adjust the resulting test scores of our white and black participants for any differences in test-taking skills
(as measured by their entering SAT scores) that may have existed between white and black
participants before the experiment. This gave us, for all intents and purposes, samples of
black and white participants with the same test-taking knowledge and skills.

tured women's underperformance in math in the laboratory, Josh and I had now captured black student underperformance in verbal reasoning in the laboratory. This result, of course, had other possible explanations. We had equated black and white participants as to their test-relevant knowledge and skill. But maybe black participants just weren't as motivated as whites to push through the frustration. Maybe they didn't take the test as seriously. Or maybe the test items were culturally biased against them. We couldn't know from this finding alone which explanation was best.

To find that out, we needed another part of the experiment that eliminated the stigma pressure blacks might feel while taking the test. As in the experiments with women and math, our challenge wasn't to figure out how to impose this pressure—that would happen automatically under ordinary testing conditions, we assumed, as soon as the test got frustrating—but how to remove it for blacks on a difficult intellectual test.

We came to a solution different from the one Steve and I had used for the women and math experiments. We used the same test on which blacks had underperformed under ordinary testing conditions. But we told a different group of participants that the test was a "task" for studying problem solving in general, and emphasized that it did not measure a person's intellectual ability. With this instruction, we made the stereotype about blacks' intelligence irrelevant to interpreting their experience on this particular "task," since it couldn't measure intellectual ability. With this instruction we freed these black participants of the stigma threat they might otherwise have experienced on a difficult test of verbal reasoning.

And they responded accordingly. They performed at the same higher level as white test takers with equal skills and knowledge, and significantly higher that the black test takers for whom the test had been presented as a test of verbal ability. With no risk of confirming the negative stereotype about their group's intelligence, any underperformance they might have shown on this test was gone, completely gone.

With this finding, we felt we knew three important things with reasonable confidence. First, we knew that the effect of stigma pressure on intellectual performance was general. It didn't happen just for women. It happened for at least two groups, women and blacks. In critical testing situations, in this society and at this time, this pressure was a contingency of these groups' identities just as much as swimming pool restrictions were a contingency of my racial identity in the Chicago of my youth. And it is a contingency with a serious toll—impaired performance on the kind of test on which one's opportunities can depend.

Second, we knew that despite the concerns of our grant reviewers and our own concerns, this contingency was powerful enough to affect the test performance of the strongest students in these groups, those with the fewest academic and motivational problems. Like the Seattle sportswriters when the Sonics began to win, we were pushed by the facts on the ground to look past the deficiencies of these groups in explaining their underperformance. More and more, it seemed that stigma pressure was involved.

And third, in finding a reliable means of reproducing in the laboratory the black student underperformance we'd seen in real life, we knew we could examine it up close—tear it apart and see how it worked. Going directly at our reasoning we had a burning question: did people experiencing stigma pressure actually worried about confirming the negative group stereotype.

We explored this in a simple way. We again asked black and white Stanford students to take a difficult verbal test. Just before the test began, we gave them a few sample test items so they could see how difficult the test would be, and then a list of eighty word fragments. Each fragment was a word with two letters missing. Their job was to complete each fragment as fast as they could, as in a free-association game. We knew from a preliminary survey that twelve of the fragments could be completed with words that reflected the stereotype about blacks' intellectual ability—for example, the fragment "—mb could be completed as "dumb" or the fragment "—ce" could be completed as "race." If simply sitting down to take a difficult test of ability was enough to make black students mindful of stereotypes about their race, these students might complete more fragments with stereotype-related words. They did. When black students were told that the test measured ability, they completed more of these fragments with stereotype-related words than when they were told the test was not a measure of ability. Being under stigma pressure clearly brought the stereotype about their group's ability to mind. Being under no such pressure during this test, whites made almost no stereotype-related completions in either case.

Josh devised another probe to find out what kind of worry the stereotype caused. Again, we asked black and white participants, just before taking the test, to make a rating, this time of their preferences for various types of music and sports. Some of these were associated with black imagery—for example, basketball, jazz, and hip-hop—and others were not—for example, swimming, tennis, and classical music. Interestingly, when black students expected to take a test of ability, they tended to spurn things black, reporting less interest in, for instance, basketball, jazz, and hip-hop than white students. But when the test was presented as unrelated to ability, black students strongly preferred things black. They seemed to be eschewing these things when preferring them would have encouraged a stereotypical view of themselves. It was the spotlight of the negative group stereotype they were avoiding.

Finally, there was evidence that the threat of the stereotype pressured a search for excuses, a search for something other than oneself to blame poor performance on. We asked participants how much sleep they'd gotten the night before the experiment. Black students expecting to take the ability test, reported getting fewer hours of sleep than black students expecting to do a nonability task, and fewer hours of sleep than whites with either expectation. At risk of a stereotype judgment, these students understandably sought some means of softening its blow should it befall them.

In addition to whatever skills and motivation they had, in addition to whatever expectations they had about being able to perform on this test, in addition to whatever capacities and tendencies they had, these black students were fending off a judgment about their group, and about themselves as members of that group. They were taking this test, and others like it, under the weight of history.

5.

These early experiments made it abundantly clear that you didn't need to have academic deficiencies to be disrupted by stigma pressure—so clear, in fact, that they raised the ironic, opposite possibility: that what makes you susceptible to stigma pressure may be less your academic deficiencies than your academic strengths! If this was so, it would be immensely important to know. It would help us better understand the nature of this pressure and whom it affects the strongest. Our experiments to that point couldn't answer these questions, because they had all included only strong students. We didn't know what would have happened had we included weaker students. Would they, too, have been affected by stigma pressure—meaning that this pressure affects everyone in the ability-stigmatized group? Or would they not have been affected by this pressure—meaning, instead, that something about being a strong student from one of these groups can make you especially susceptible to this pressure? To answer these questions all we needed was a sample of weaker students from one of the groups we had studied. Then we could redo the experiment and see whether stigma pressure impaired their performance as it had the performance of stronger students from the group. We had only one problem: where to find a sample of weaker students on the highly selective university campus we were on.

Sometimes opportunity walks right through the door—not often enough, but sometimes. Not long after our early experiments were published, a new graduate student, Joseph Brown, and an undergraduate student he had met while working as a teaching assistant, Mikel Jollet, asked whether they could see me. They made an interesting pair—Joseph, a slender, scholarly, African American graduate student with wire-rimmed glasses who had actually read all the books you wish you had, and Mikel, a highly energetic, hip-hop-style college student who bubbled with confidence and entrepreneurial spirit. (In fact, Mikel was to become, in his not-too-distant future, the lead singer of the highly successful rock band the Airborne Toxic Event.) They were interested in the experiment that Josh and I had done, showing the effect of the racial stereotype on the test performance of black Stanford students. They had a question. Would the same thing have happened if we'd done the experiment in the inner-city Los Angeles high school that Mikel had graduated from three years earlier? As important, they had an opportunity. Mikel was still in contact with his former teachers at the high school. He thought they'd let him try the experiment there. Opportunity knocked.

In no time, armed with packets of experimental materials, Mikel was on a plane to Los Angeles to redo in his old high school the same experiment that Josh and I had done at Stanford. It would be his undergraduate honors thesis. He gave a difficult thirty-minute test (a section of the SAT verbal exam) to groups of white and black students in spare classrooms. For those groups in which he wanted black students to experience the pressure of the racial stereotype, he did as Josh and I had done; he simply said the test was a test of verbal ability. Remember, this minimal statement reminds blacks that this is a test on which their performance could confirm the standing stereotype about their group's intellectual ability. For groups in which he wanted black students to experience no pressure from this racial stereotype, he again did as Josh and had done; he described the test as an instrument to study problem solving in general, not one that was "diagnostic" of individual differences in ability. This made the stereotype about blacks' ability irrelevant to their performance on the task, since, ostensibly, the task wasn't about the thing the stereotype was about (intellectual ability).

Then he did something that Josh and I didn't do. He measured how much his student participants cared about school, how much they identified with being good students. What he found was interesting, and made vivid the irony we had suspected all along. For the half of his participants who cared most about school, Mikel found just what Josh and I had found. Black students performed dramatically worse than equally skilled white students when the test was presented as an ability test, when they were at risk of confirming the negative ability stereotype about their group; but they performed just as well as equally skilled whites when the test was presented as nondiagnostic of intellectual ability, when they were at no risk of confirming the ability stereotype. Blacks in the academic vanguard of Mikel's inner-city high school reacted just like black Stanford students. They were disrupted by the possibility of confirming the negative stereotype about their group's ability. But this didn't happen for blacks in the academic rear guard of Mikel's high school sample. The black test takers who cared less about school were unfazed by the stereotype. They performed the same regardless of whether the test was presented as an ability test or as a nondiagnostic laboratory task. And in both of these groups, they performed at the same level as white students who, like them, didn't care much about achieving in school and didn't have strong skills.

Before concluding that not caring about school is a good remedy for the pressure of negative ability stereotypes, we have to note a big hitch—none of these rearguard students did that well on the test. The rearguard black students performed no worse under stereotype pressure than under no stereotype pressure. But, like their white rearguard counterparts, they performed badly in both situations. They simply lacked the skills and motivation to do well. They behaved cooperatively enough. They took the test politely. But when it got difficult, not caring very much, they gave up, looked at the clock on the wall, and waited for the session to be over.

When most people think about the poor school achievement of minority students, they think about Mikel's rearguard students, who have weaker skills and motivation and who are apt to be already alienated from school. To an observer trying to explain their poor test performance, like the Seattle sportswriters trying to explain the faltering Sonics of early 1978, there are deficiencies galore to hang one's hat on—poor prior schooling, distressed communities, the psychic damage of self-doubt and low expectations, a resulting alienation from school, poor academic skills, more school alienation, possible lack of family support, alienating peer cultures, and so on. Any or all of these things could have been behind their giving up and performing badly in Mikel's experiment. For these students, the conventional wisdom seemed right.

The conventional wisdom wasn't right, though, for the vanguard students, the students who had somehow survived these problems to become identified with school even though they were in an inner-city high school. The only thing depressing their performance in Mikel's experiment was the pressure of the negative stereotype—the risk of confirming it, or of being seen to confirm it. It was the same pressure that depressed the test performance of the black students at Stanford, and the same pressure that depressed the math test performance of the strong women math students at Michigan. When that pressure was removed—by presenting the test as a laboratory task—they performed at the top of their skill level.

Here was the irony we had suspected. What made Mikel's vanguard black students susceptible to stereotype pressure was not weaker academic confidence and skills but stronger academic confidence and skills. Their strengths led them to be identified with school, to care about school and how well they did. But in school, when working on difficult material they understood to be ability diagnostic, they encountered the extra pressure of the stereotype. It wasn't low expectations that made them susceptible to this pressure, then; it was high expectations.

Mikel's experiment showed something else, too. It showed why this extra pressure is hard to see down on the ground of everyday schooling: the black vanguard students, under stereotype pressure, performed at the same low level as the black rearguard students who lacked the skills to perform better regardless of how much pressure they were under. The test performance of the two groups was indistinguishable. It would be easy to miss then—when interpreting these scores from the perspective of a classroom teacher or, even more distantly, from that of an admissions committee—the point that the poor performance of these two groups had different causes. One sector of these students was like the 1978 Sonics in the early part of the season. They might not have been perfect, but they had the skills and motivation to win—in this case, to perform like the academic vanguard they were. All they needed was relief from the pressure of a stereotype.

6.

Though in some ways just beginning, this had been, by then, a research journey of four or so years. And throughout the whole of it we'd gotten no evidence that the underperformance we'd observed came from characteristics of the person who was underperforming. It seemed, instead, to come from the pressure of group stereotypes they had to deal with on tests or in classrooms. We came to think of this pressure as a "predicament" of identity. An American woman in an advanced college math class knows at some level that she could be seen as limited because she is a woman; a black student knows the same thing in almost any challenging academic setting; and a white elite sprinter knows it, too, as he reaches the last 10 meters of a 100-meter race. These people know their group identity. They know how their society views it. They know they are doing something for which that view is relevant. They know, at some level, that they are in a predicament: their performance could confirm a bad view of their group and of themselves, as members of the group.

Over the years we used several working names for this predicament—"stigmatization," "stigma pressure," "stigma vulnerability," "stereotype vulnerability." Eventually we settled on "stereotype threat." This term captured the idea of a situational predicament as a contingency of their group identity, a real threat of judgment or treatment in the person's environment that went beyond any limitations within.

7.

We had gotten to an understanding of stereotype threat by trying to understand women's and minorities' underperformance in school. In the process, we discovered a predicament that affected everyone in one form or another, to one degree or another, in one place or another, and not occasionally but frequently. One thing I liked about this fact was that it gave everyone a chance to see into other groups' experience. The stereotype threat that blacks felt in taking a standardized test resembles the stereotype threat that women felt in taking a difficult math test. Analogy is often the best route to empathic insight. One's own stereotype threat can analogize one into understanding the other guy's stereotype threat.

The reality of stereotype threat also made the point that places like classrooms, university campuses, standardized-testing rooms, or competitive-running tracks, though seemingly the same for everybody, are, in fact, different places for different people. Depending on their group identity, different people would simply have different things to contend with in these places—different stereotype threats, different ambiguities about how to interpret their experience, different goals and preoccupations.

For women in advanced college chemistry, for black students in school in general, for older people returning to school, for white sprinters in elite sprinting, there are stereotypes "loose in the house" that make these situations different for them than for people from other groups. Their persistence in these situations, then, might come up against different calculations. For example, when the young talented white sprinter is deciding whether or not to persist in sprinting, he is deciding to persist in a situation that is fundamentally different from the situation that a young talented black sprinter is deciding to persist in. On a daily basis, as long as he remains in sprinting, he will have to contend with the threat of being negatively stereotyped. And the threat will come at the worst time: in the most pressured situations, when he is at greatest risk of confirming the stereotype about his group's abilities.

Beneath the particulars of our research, a background story was emerging. To improve the achievement gaps that launched our research, as well as to know better how we all function, we needed to better understand our social identities and how they work in our lives. Especially in America, perhaps, we stress individuality. We resist seeing ourselves as circumscribed by social identities—our being older, black, white male, religious, politically liberal, and so on. This is probably a good resistance. It pushes us beyond the constraints of identity. Still, our research was revealing a profound importance of social identity: that the contingencies that go with them in specific places at specific times, while often subtle enough to be beneath our awareness, can nonetheless significantly affect things as important as our intellectual functioning. It also suggested, in turn, that these effects might play a significant role in the underperformance in school and on standardized tests of major groups in our society.

These revelations have sparked considerable further research in my lab and in many others as well. Major questions have been explored: What kind of behaviors and capacities does this threat interfere with? What does stereotype threat do to a person that causes this interference? What makes this threat strong or weak? And what can individuals and institutions do to reduce its unwanted effects?

But beneath all of this work is a broadened conception of how

our social identities shape who we are, what we do, and how well
we do it. The through-line of this book follows this research program in its march toward finding remedies for the ill effects of this
threat. And some remarkable remedies do emerge. At this point,
however, it might be helpful to briefly step off this through-line
for a closer look at this broadened conception of social identity and
its role in our lives.*

---

*The findings discussed in this chapter might lead to the view that stereotype threat is
less of a factor in the performance of stereotyped students in weaker schools with fewer
caring students. This could prove correct. But these findings also show that there are
academically caring students in even less advantaged schools—students who can be very
much affected by stereotype threat. Also, virtually everyone cares about some intellectual
behaviors—speaking well to teachers or in class, for example—and stereotype threat
should affect these behaviors even among weaker students in weaker schools.

CHAPTER 4

———— ▄ ————

A Broader View of Identity: In the Lives of Anatole Broyard, Amin Maalouf, and the Rest of Us

As our findings came in, I remember struggling to absorb their meaning. As you have seen, they persistently suggested that our social identities influence us, in big part, through the conditions we get exposed to because we have the identity—conditions that might range from swimming pool restrictions to stereotype threat. Our findings offered this interpretation, but I still found it a bit foreign. Perhaps it was because I am a psychologist. Psychologists focus on the internal, the psychological. If women underperform on a difficult math test, our tendency is to look for a characteristic internal to women that could cause it—the observer's perspective again, this time arising from my discipline. I needed more fleshed-out images of just how contingencies of social identity worked in real life. If I could see that, then maybe I could be more persuaded by the direction our explanations were taking.

I was thinking about this when, one day, I picked up a *New Yorker* magazine article by Henry Louis Gates Jr. entitled "White like Me: African American Author Anatole Broyard." I knew as I read along that I was seeing what I needed to see, a real-life version of the processes revealed in our experiments—a man's life in explicit negotiation with some of our history's most powerful identity contingencies. To illustrate, I'll tell here a little of his story.

1.

Anatole Broyard was the daily book reviewer for the *New York Times* for eighteen years, as well as a consistent contributor to the *New York Times Book Review*. He also wrote stories and essays that appeared in spurts throughout his career, the last spurt of which was a beautiful series of essays on illness that appeared before his death in 1990 of prostate cancer. I had read his work for years, but I was especially impressed with the illness essays. They were funny, erudite, profound. If their charm had a formula, it came from Broyard's ability to mix sophisticated literary allusions and street-hip images of modern life with concrete descriptions of managing his illness. There were even elements of the stand-up comic, a comic with the erudition of an English professor talking about life, decline, and death. He reminded me of Saul Bellow, but more Freudian. I had the vague impression he was Jewish, and probably European. Who knew what I was picking up on—his name perhaps, his style of humor. But, mind you, I never thought much about it until I picked up that *New Yorker* magazine in 1996. In it Gates revealed that Broyard was black, that both of his parents were black, and that all of his ancestors were black as far back as the eighteenth century.

I wasn't the only one to have this misconception. Broyard had lived a deception. Though black in every conventional meaning of the term, he had lived his adult life as white. That is, he had "passed"—as it's called in the black community—never revealing his black identity, not even to his children, until just before his death.

Broyard and his immediate family—his mother, father, and two sisters—were part of the Great Migration of blacks from the South to the urban North during the early and mid-twentieth century. For the Broyards, this meant a move from New Orleans to the Bedford Stuyvesant section of Brooklyn. Migration, by definition, involves people leaving the communities in which they and their families are known for new communities in which they and their families are unknown, very likely. It is a move in which, if one has the physical appearance to pull it off, one can leave one's racial identity behind. During the 1920s, the peak years of the Great Migration, it is estimated that ten to thirty thousand blacks shed their black identities each year in precisely this way, passing into a sea of whiteness as they migrated north. Broyard's own father, Paul Broyard, was a practitioner of passing, but only during the workday. He was a highly skilled carpenter. He "passed" as white during the day so that he could join the carpenter's union and get work. At the end of the day, he went back home to a family that, by all accounts, was comfortably black. Revealing both the severity and the absurdity of the color line in that era, this form of daytime passing was then common among light-skinned blacks. The young Anatole had role models, even a close role model, in how to handle the peculiar institution of the American color line.

There's a joke people tell about Michael Jackson: "Only in America could a poor little black boy grow up to become a rich white woman." Broyard never really got rich (or mistaken for a woman), but he did make the other part of that journey. As a boy growing up he was black, as a student at Boys High School in Brooklyn and at Brooklyn College. It was during this time that he fell in love with literature, European and American, and with both high and popular culture. He wanted to be a writer, a great American writer, and he brought a lot to the table: knowledge of city life through his Brooklyn upbringing, all to be blended with a precocious literary erudition.

Toward the end of World War II, and still living black, Broyard married a black woman. They had a child. He joined the army. It was apparently during his time there—who knows in reaction to what—that Broyard decided to renegotiate his racial identity. The particulars are murky. But when he came out of the army he left his wife and child for Greenwich Village in New York City. There the little black boy from Brooklyn resumed life under a different cover. Anatole Broyard had become white.

In the Village he became a local raconteur, published essays, bought a bookstore, became a writing teacher at the New School for Social Research and New York University, published another spurt of essays, married a white woman, got a huge book contract to write an autobiographical novel (which he never finished), got hired by the New York Times as its daily book reviewer, and eventually moved to the suburbs in Connecticut, where his chosen social identity could be even safer from his given social identity.

Broyard could have struggled against the limiting conditions of his life as a black man. But because he had the opportunity, and I am sure for a mix of other reasons, he decided not to. And when he changed his racial identity, he changed the contingencies that went with it—the constraints he had to face, the opportunities he would be given, the pathways he could go down. He would be met with different expectations. He could live in different places—the West Village as opposed to being segregated in Bedford Stuyvesant or Harlem. He could have access to different resources, such as a bank loan to buy or lease a bookstore and a professional network that could yield a job offer from the New York Times, neither of which he could ever have had if he had remained black. He could know different people. He could marry different people. His children could have access to different schools. He could become a different kind of writer. As a white man he walked the same streets in the West Village he had walked as a black man. His society had the same laws and institutions. He himself had the same talents, weaknesses, psychological traits, cultural beliefs, the same preferences, attitudes, values, and so on. All of this was the same. What differed was his social identity. He was now a white man, not a black man. His social location was different. From this location, the pathways his life could take were completely different.

We typically think of race as rooted in essences—possibly biological, possibly cultural—that are intrinsic and defining. But Broyard's story of passing, like thousands of other stories of passing, frustrates this tendency. Nothing of his essence, biological or cultural, changed when he passed into the white world. He was the same person. What differed were the conditions he faced.

In our terms, he had exchanged one set of identity contingencies for another—those that went with being black in that place and time for those that went with being white in that place and time. And with this exchange, his life changed.

As I've said, I am a psychologist with a psychologist's bias—that of looking inside people for the causes of their behavior and achievements. But both our own research, showing how the stereotype threat that goes with certain social identities in school and on tests can dramatically affect intellectual performance, and the Broyard story, showing in real life how changing a social identity can lead to completely different conditions of life, were strengthening my conviction in the idea of identity contingencies—that they are real and that they may be underappreciated as causes of our actions and outcomes.

2.

I borrowed the admittedly jargonistic term "contingencies" from behaviorism, the approach that dominated scientific psychology throughout much of the twentieth century. It refers to those conditions in a setting that reward some behaviors and punish others, and thereby determine how we respond in the setting and what we learn. These contingencies are called response contingencies in behaviorism. In the sense that I am using the term, contingencies are conditions you have to deal with in a setting in order to function in it. And identity contingencies are contingencies that are special to you because you have a given social identity, things like the availability of a bank loan to Broyard only when he was white, or the lowered expectations for mental alertness one might experience as an older person, or the social avoidance a southerner might experience as his accent is heard at a New England cocktail party. These are identity contingencies.

They arise from the way a setting is organized around identity and from the way identities in the setting are stereotyped. Think about the typical American high school cafeteria, where seating is famously segregated by race. Imagine the identity contingencies this poses for a white student and a black student as they enter—contingencies they know all too well simply by knowing the school culture and the larger society. The white student knows, for example, that if he sits with the black students he could be judged in unsavory ways—as trying too hard to be cool, as being inauthentic perhaps, as being racially insensitive, and so on. He could worry that he'd get a frosty reception, that he'd say something that would be taken the wrong way, that he'd miss cultural references. The black student knows the contingencies of his identity in the cafeteria too. He knows that if he sits with the white students, other black students could see him as disloyal, as wanting to be white perhaps. He could worry that the white students wouldn't understand the pressures he feels at school, that he couldn't be open about them without making them feel blamed. He could worry that being himself would risk disapproval. Both identities have heavy contingencies in this lunchroom, contingencies that bring the racial history of this nation into the everyday experience of these students. To explain the lunchroom's racial segregation, one needn't postulate even an iota of group prejudice on the part of any student in the room. Its segregation could arise solely to avoid the bad contingencies of these two group identities in that place.

You can see the theme here. As in politics, all identities are local. They stem from local particulars, local contingencies.

3.

Yet, as this (contingency-based) view of social identity was developing, I sensed that something implicit in our thinking needed to be made explicit. I noticed that most of the identity contingencies I could think of that were capable of influencing us—our thoughts, feelings, and actions—were contingencies that either threatened the person, as in the case of stereotype threat, or restricted the person's access to opportunity, like swimming pool restrictions. The identity contingencies that made the biggest difference in our functioning seemed to threaten or restrict us in some way.

This idea was in the back of my mind when I got back to my Stanford office after a lecture I'd given at the Radcliffe Institute in Cambridge, Massachusetts, and opened my email. The Radcliffe Institute used to be Radcliffe College, the distinguished women's college affiliated with Harvard University and located just off Harvard Square. Now it's a distinguished institute for advanced study, where internationally prominent scholars and scientists pursue projects for a year. My audience, however, was largely students from Harvard and Boston-area colleges. I talked about social identities and the contingencies that went with them. To stress the multiplicity of our social identities, I listed nine of them on a PowerPoint slide, identities like age, sex, sexual orientation, race, profession, nationality, and political affiliation. I thought this enumeration was fairly comprehensive. But when I flew back to California that night and opened the email, the following message was waiting for me:

> Today I had the pleasure of hearing your speech at Radcliffe on Stereotypes and Identity. [So far, I liked it.] I am a Stanford graduate (1998) who suffers from bipolar disorder. I related to a lot of the talk of contingencies and such in this way. Even when I am healthy, I worry that I will be thought of as crazy. I spend much of my time passing for a "normal" society member. However, when I go to a manic-depressive support group, I feel more free and become more open. Yet, I couldn't say this in the question and answer session, for God forbid I should be interviewed at some point in my life for a job from people who heard me speak, and I could be discriminated against. It consumes me whether or not to share this information about my disorder with people I live with (I now live in a house for people with psychiatric disorders, so right now that's easier) or to people I know in other ways, including my family. Mental health status was not mentioned in your list of race, religion, etc. It is often left out. However, I took that as a cue, as you called them, that I was not included, that my disorder was more than could even make the list. Please feel free to share my story with others without using my name. . . .

I was glad the student ended with that permission. Here was a glimpse into the experience of social identity threat.

It's not a focused threat. It's not focused on a particular bad thing that could happen. This student didn't know what could happen, didn't even know whether anything would happen, and certainly didn't know, if something did happen, where or when it would happen. She knew only that something could happen, on the basis of her bipolar identity. Negative contingencies were easy to imagine—immediate embarrassment and humiliation if the identity was revealed to this audience, to her friends, even to her family, the possibility of social rejection, awkward interactions, lost career opportunities, of being judged, of being dismissed.

Identity threat is diffuse—as I've said, like a snake loose in the house. Our bipolar student has to remain vigilant to her social world, combing over it for evidence of how people feel about people who are bipolar. Where will the snake be? How bad is its bite? Will she lose a job or educational opportunities, be shunned, and so on?

A diffuse threat is preoccupying. And it preoccupies one with the identity it threatens. This is the point that had to be made explicit: identity threat—the subset of identity contingencies that actually threaten the person in some way—is a primary way by which an identity takes hold of us, in the sense of shaping how we function and even in telling us that we have a particular identity. In the auditorium that day, a perfectly normal-appearing college graduate, a person who fit seamlessly into the surroundings, was nonetheless preoccupied with her bipolar identity. Identity threat, diffuse and Delphic though it may be, is nonetheless powerful enough to single out an identity and make it the center of a person's functioning, powerful enough to make it more important, for the duration of the threat at least, than any of the person's other identities—more important than her sex, her race, her religion, her being young, her being a Stanford graduate.

4.

The French essayist and novelist Amin Maalouf is a man of many social identities. Born a Christian in Lebanon with Arabic as his mother tongue, he was sent to a French Jesuit school as a boy. In 1976, fleeing war in his homeland, he emigrated to France, where he began a writing career in French and where he has lived ever since. So, at the very least, Maalouf is Lebanese, French, Arab, Catholic, a writer, a male, and an émigré all at the same time. Perhaps it was this multiplicity of identities that enabled him to write a deeply perceptive book entitled *In the Name of Identity: Violence and the Need to Belong*. The book's central question resounds deeply in our times: "[W]hy do so many people commit crimes [and violence] in the name of identity?" Its answer is that, in the name of an identity that one sees as under siege, one can do things that one could never do as an individual, things that one could never do in one's own name. In defense of one's country, one's religion, one's region, one's ethnicity, the image of one's group in the world, one can do things that would otherwise be unimaginable. *In the Name of Identity* offers a powerful thesis, which illuminates the outbreaks of terrorism, war, and genocide that so plague modern life. And in the process, it describes the power of identity threat to lay claim to our psyches:

> People often see themselves in terms of whichever one of their allegiances [identities] is most under attack. And sometimes, when a person doesn't have the strength to defend that allegiance, he hides it. Then it remains buried deep down in the dark, await-

ing its revenge. But whether he accepts or conceals it, proclaims it discreetly or flaunts it, it is with that allegiance that the person concerned identifies. *And then, whether it relates to colour, religion, language or class, it invades the person's whole identity.* Other people who share the same allegiance sympathise; they all gather together, join forces, encourage one another, challenge "the other side." (p. 26, italics added)

Maalouf's emphasis is similar to mine: of all the things that make an identity prominent in one's feeling and thinking, being threatened on the basis of it is perhaps the most important. It was threat of public exposure, of lost relationships and jobs that led the student in my audience to assert her bipolar identity. This threat makes the identity to which it is directed, of all the person's social identities, the one that dominates emotion, thinking, the one that, for that time "invades the person's whole identity."

For Maalouf, then, as for me, threatening identity contingencies have the greatest power. Being *threatened* because we have a given characteristic is what makes us most aware of being a particular *kind* of person.

To see this in your own life, think of the important settings in your life, your school, your workplace, your family. The argument, put most strongly, is that if there is nothing in these settings that you have to deal with because you are a woman, or older, or black, or have a Spanish accent, then these characteristics—being a woman, being older, being black, or having a Spanish accent—will not become important social identities for you in that setting. They'll be characteristics you have. You may cherish them for a variety of reasons. But in that setting they won't much affect how you see things, whom you identify with, how you react emotionally to events in the setting, whom you relate to easily, and so on. They won't become central to who you are there.

I am thus proposing something simple: the sense of having a given social identity arises from having to deal with important identity contingencies, usually threatening or restrictive contingencies like negative stereotypes about your group, group segregations of one sort or another, discrimination and prejudice, and so on, all because you have a given characteristic. What raises a characteristic we have to a social identity we have are the contingencies that go with the characteristic, most often, threatening contingencies.

Tell me, when I was seven or eight, that I should be more interested in my African American heritage, and I might have listened with modest interest—for a while anyway. But keep me out of a swimming pool because of it, and even at seven or eight, I became consumed with the identity. It was never the burden for me that it was for Broyard. I was of a later generation. I was exposed to different racial contingencies over most of the important situations of my life, and to powerful positive things about this identity, about the people who had lived under its contingencies. This identity influences many things about me—tastes, preferences, perspectives, my sense of self. But I'd be foolish not to remember that the whole consciousness and personhood that goes with it began with a contingency of this identity, the fact of swimming on Wednesdays and sitting home the rest of the week.

Identities do have positive and neutral contingencies too— things one confronts in society because one has a given identity that are not threatening, but just neutral or even positive. Men have to go to men's bathrooms and women to women's bathrooms. This arrangement is indeed a contingency, of sexual identity. Yet it is so routine as to be essentially neutral. We don't notice it. A contingency as neutral as this doesn't make us see, feel, and experience the world in terms of our sexual identity. (Unless we mistakenly go into the wrong bathroom or unless we have an androgynous appearance. Then sex-typed bathrooms could constitute a negative identity contingency that would make one highly aware of one's own sexual identity.)

Positive identity contingencies, too, may do little to make us identity-aware. When people are choosing sides for pickup basketball, I might get chosen early because I am African American and because, in this society, African Americans are positively stereotyped in basketball. Yet because being chosen early disrupts nothing for me, I might not notice it. I might not notice I had an advantage. I might assume I was evaluated the same as everyone else. And not noticing my advantage, I might not become much aware of the identity on which it was based.

So the kind of contingency most likely to press an identity on you is a threatening one, the threat of something *bad* happening to you because you have the identity. You don't have to be sure it will happen. It's enough that it *could* happen. It's the possibility that requires vigilance and that makes the identity preoccupying.

The bipolar student in my audience couldn't put the question aside. She wanted to know. "How could a man who makes a living studying predicaments of identity fail to mention mine?" "Is being bipolar so bad that it can't be mentioned?" She was reading cues, figuring out the meaning of her identity and how it would affect her life. Even though her identity was concealed, these questions couldn't be taken lightly.

James Comer is the innovator of one of the nation's most successful school reform programs. Time and again, careful implementation of his strategies has transformed poorly performing public schools into outstanding schools, with dramatic elevations in student test scores. He knows that low-income minority students can suffer, among other things, the kind of identity threat I describe. To help alleviate it, he sometimes gives a simple piece of advice. If something happens that might reflect prejudice or unfairness against people from their neighborhood, he tells them, they should ignore it. If it happens again, he tells them they should ignore it. If it happens a third time, he tells them, they should raise all hell. Comer's advice is a strategy of probabilities. Chances are the first cue that could be a sign of race or class prejudice isn't a sign of prejudice. I remember that Jim and I amused ourselves with speculation: Were 30 percent of these first cues innocent? 70 percent? Was the percentage changing? It's impossible to put a hard number on it. What I liked about his advice was what it illustrated about the psychic burden of the students—that it was, in big part, a worry born of ambiguity, a worry about whether their race and class might affect how they were seen, a worry about identity contingencies. His advice, if they could make it a habit of mind, raises the threshold for how much ambiguity is worth worrying about. Until things become clearer, they can move concerns about identity to the back burner.

For the most part, then, it is threat that allows a given identity to "invade [our] whole identity." My examples show this in relation to serious threats: possible lost jobs, social rejection, public embarrassment, and the like. But are contingencies this serious necessary to make an identity central to our functioning? One of the most dramatic research traditions in social psychology is dramatic precisely because it consistently shows the opposite: that even the most minimal identity threats are enough to make us think and behave like a group member.

5.

In the summer of 1969, shortly after taking a chaired professorship at the University of Bristol in England, the world-famous social psychologist Henri Tajfel, with the help of Michael Billig, M. G.

Bundy, and Claude Flament, brought sixty-four boys, fourteen and fifteen years old, into his new Bristol laboratory in groups of eight. They told the boys that the experiment was about visual judgments and asked them to judge the number of dots in forty-dot clusters flashed on a screen in front them. Ostensibly based on these estimates, each boy was then told that he was either an "over-estimator" or an "under-estimator." In fact, these labels were assigned randomly.

Next, the boys were taken to separate cubicles and asked to assign points worth small amounts of money to two other boys. To make these assignments, they were given a table of allocation choices. Each choice was set up so that it gave one boy more points than the other boy. Would the boys favor boys in their own group even though their "group"—being an "over-estimator" or an "under-estimator"—was essentially meaningless?

The unsettling answer is yes. When the boys chose allocations between two boys in their own group, they allocated as equally as the table of choices would allow. But when the boys made allocations between a boy in their own "estimator" group and a boy in the other "estimator" group, they invariably favored the boy in their own group. They discriminated in favor of even this minimal identity.

A second study divided another group of similarly aged boys into groups on the basis of their preference for a painting by either Klee or Kandinsky, two early twentieth-century European painters of quite similar style and technique. Again, the boys made allocations. But this time the tables they were given made them choose an overall strategy of allocation: one that always allocated points equally between boys of the two groups; one that always maximized the joint profit of boys from both groups; and one that always maximized the profit of boys from their group over boys from the other group, even when doing so would net "their" boy fewer points than a more equitable strategy.

Again, the boys discriminated. When choosing between maximizing profit for both boys and maximizing profit for the boy from their group over the boy from the other group, they chose to maximize the advantage of the boy from their own group, *even when this strategy gave that boy less money than he would have gotten in a more equitable allocation.* These young boys from Oxford were a competitive lot. They sacrificed profit for group advantage, even though the group they advantaged was made up on an essentially random basis.

And lest you think that only young Oxfordians would behave this way, it's important to stress that in the thirty-five years since these findings were first published, they have been replicated over a thousand times, in hundreds of different samples of people, in dozens of countries of the world. No type of person or nation of people has shown immunity to this "minimal group effect," as it is now called.

Why do we discriminate so easily? Tajfel and his student John Turner posited a simple answer: self-esteem. We think well of our group in order to think well of ourselves—even when the group is "minimal," a passing group, like being an underestimator of dots. When the group is more important, such as the high school we went to, the process is even easier to see. We think well of our high school as part of thinking well of ourselves. This would hold, of course, for all kinds of groups and affiliations—our neighborhood, city, age cohort, income level, and so on. And in liking our groups as part of liking ourselves, we just might favor members of our group over members of other groups—the need for self-esteem driving in-group favoritism. It would happen without our being much aware of it. But it seems to happen.

The experiments of Tajfel and his colleagues made several profound points that weren't obvious to the naked eye: that our need for self-regard was powerful enough to make us care about even trivial group identities; that we could discriminate against other people about whom we knew nothing except that they weren't members of a group we were part of, even when the group was trivial; and that all of this is true for virtually everyone on earth (although there is evidence that it is less true for people from collective societies).

How easy it is to ignite human bias. Nothing special about either the perpetrator or the victim is required. Ordinary human functioning—maintaining one's self-esteem—is enough. This was a revelation about the human psyche.

And in showing the minimal conditions needed for group prejudice, Tajfel also showed the minimal conditions needed for a sense of group identity. To feel a given identity, to have that identity take hold of us and affect how we function, the contingencies tied to it needn't be dramatic or even consequential. "Minimal" threats will do the job. It's enough to be classified an "over-estimator"—a minimal threat, to be sure, but enough of a threat to activate an identity, to make it, for a time at least, "pervade the whole identity." When it comes to identity threat, we humans are a sensitive lot.

6.

Not long ago I heard an interview conducted by Ira Glass during an episode of National Public Radio's *This American Life* that had a pointed relevance to a central implication of our thinking. The implication is this: if our social identities—our racial, sexual, or political identities, for example—are substantially rooted in local contingencies, as much as or more than in internal traits, they might not travel well. That is, our sense of being a certain kind of person, and our functioning like a certain kind of person, might be more variable from one context to the next than we would think.

Our evolving reasoning implied this. Our experiments had shown that it could happen. Women and blacks underperformed when they were under the identity contingency of stereotype threat, but not when that contingency was removed. The impact their identities had on them changed dramatically from one situation to the next. Still, I worried. It's just difficult to imagine that a change in setting could change the degree to which a given social identity "pervades the whole identity." Could we find phenomena that illustrate a significant malleability of social identity in real life? Finding one would encourage our thinking. Sometimes in problem solving it's not "my kingdom for a horse" but "my kingdom for a good example." And this is where the Ira Glass interview comes in.

The program focused on the question "Why do so many Americans love Paris?" One of Glass's interests was in African American expatriation—the long tradition of expatriation to Paris by African American writers and artists, like James Baldwin, Josephine Baker, Richard Wright, and countless jazz musicians. This is a fabled community dating back to the early twentieth century. Tours of it are offered to this day. Glass asked a young African American woman who had been living in Paris for several years whether African American expatriation was still what it had been cracked up to be.

She began her answer with a description of her life in the United States. She was born in Brooklyn and raised there in a housing project. She was a good student, which hadn't always helped with her peers. She got into a good college and hoped for a better school experience. But there, too, she had problems fitting in. The middle-class black women she tried to befriend saw her as a "project girl." She saw them as "putting the 'B' in 'bougie.'" Tension persisted. Neither were white women a recourse; they, she said, just didn't have much to do with her. And then there was the larger context of race relations in the United States. Our society, reflecting its history and ongoing ways of life, is still sufficiently organized by race to create contingencies of identity for all of us—especially, perhaps, for a black woman from a Brooklyn housing project.

Then, a plane ride to Paris. She went on a lark, but finding it beautiful and comfortable, she moved in, got work, tackled the language seriously, and committed to it her indefinite future.

Ira Glass asked her about her experience of race in Paris. Her mood elevated; a happiness came through. She said she is still black in Paris, but it isn't the most central thing about her when she meets people. Her blackness, she said, especially as an educated black person, doesn't mean the same thing to people in Paris that it does in the United States. She described Parisians' affection for African Americans, their romance with jazz and African American writers. She says she is met first as a full person in Paris.

She noted quickly that the French are no less prejudiced than anyone else. She described their lack of affection for North African immigrants, former colonials—many of whom look like her. She remarked that her American-accented French helps her avoid being confused as North African. She said the relationship between the French and North Africans has similarities to that between white and black Americans, but that French society is even less open to incorporating its minorities than American society. She said that no matter how good her French gets, she will never be taken in as fully French.

Nonetheless, she said that sometimes riding on the subway she finds herself, beneath her breath, thanking the French for letting her live in their country. She said that she feels at home in Paris and that, in all likelihood, she won't repatriate to the States.

All identities are local, I have been arguing, rooted in local contingencies. When this woman went to Paris, she changed identity contingencies. And with the change, the psychological, everyday importance of her identities changed. In Paris being a black American had considerably less importance to her everyday life. Occasionally, it could even elicit affection. Moreover, she'd left her "project girl" identity, and its conflict with "bougie" girls, completely behind. Absolutely nothing she had to deal with in her Parisian life related to these identities. No contingencies, no identity is the argument. As Glass put it, the central, defining identity conflict of her life in America simply vanished in Paris.

She had achieved there much of what Broyard had achieved by passing. In passing you change your race but keep your country. In expatriation you keep your race but change your country. These strategies are different sides of the same coin—the pursuit of less limiting contingencies of identity.

This is not to say that this African American in Paris had no vestiges of her African American identity. Vestiges would surely remain: preferences for hamburgers and BBQ, for baseball, for the way Americans smile more and say hello, for certain kinds of music, and so on. She might take great pleasure in the company of other American expatriates. But these internal dispositions from her African American identity would be less pertinent to her new life and might even fade with time.

Looking over her shoulder as she talked, I wondered what line is drawn when you can't be taken in as "French." Does it mean you can't run for office, can't be part of the professional class, can't be a doctor or a professor? It also occurred to me that expatriation is not a tactic you can easily retreat from. To come back from Paris, our expatriate would have to learn the contemporary American contingencies of her old identities, of her gender identity, her racial identity. Contingencies change. The longer she stays away, the more she would have to learn in order to return. Expatriation carries the risk of getting stranded in the new identity. Passing carries this risk too. This may be why it was so difficult for Broyard to reveal his racial identity to his children. Doing so would have committed him to repatriation, to forging some new black identity against new black contingencies. His wife, Sandy, told Gates that she would periodically plead with Broyard to tell the children. He steadfastly refused. The rigors of "coming home"—learning how to handle the new contingencies of his old identity as a black—would have been formidable, especially for one so visible.

These thoughts occurred to me as I listened to the Glass interview of the African American expatriate in Paris. But if they occurred to her, she wasn't yet bothered by them.

The experiments that my colleagues and I were doing showed that something generally thought to emanate from an internal capacity associated with social identity—as the level of women's math performance might emanate from women's math ability— could be changed dramatically by changing contingencies of that identity, by changing, in this research, the degree to which test takers were at risk of confirming bad stereotypes about their group. And the phenomena of identity change—"passing" and expatriation- —suggested that what we were seeing in the lab was the tip of an iceberg, an outcropping of a more fundamental fact about social identity. They suggested that the degree to which a given social identity had any presence in a person's life depended on contin- gencies, realities down on the ground that the person had to deal with because they had the identity. Take these contingencies away by allowing the person to "pass," or change these contingencies by allowing the person to expatriate out of them, and the whole identity could fall to irrelevance. A relocation to Paris, and a life- defining identity conflict vanishes.

What did this say about social identity? What did it say about what would have to be remedied in order to make progress on the problems that began our research? Two conclusions seemed unavoidable. First, our social identities are adaptations to the particular circumstances of our lives, what I am calling identity contingencies. If we didn't need them to help us cope with these circumstances, the perspectives, emotional tendencies, values, ambitions, and habits that make up the dispositional side of our social identities would just gradually leak out of our psyches and be gone. The second conclusion foreshadows the more pragmatic direction this book is taking. If you want to change the behaviors and outcomes associated with social identity—say, too few women in computer science—don't focus on changing the internal manifestations of the identity, such as values, and attitudes. Focus instead on changing the contingencies to which all of that internal stuff is an adaptation. Bert Williams, the great African American comedian of the early twentieth century, once said, "I have never been able to discover that there is anything disgraceful about being a Negro, but I have to concede, I have found it inconvenient." In Williams's terms, then, we needn't worry about changing something "disgraceful" about being a Negro; change instead the "inconvenience" of being a Negro, change the contingencies of the identity.

Although our broadening understanding of social identity seemed promising, the game of science is played on the ground, as they say, on the ground of empirical research. And this broadening understanding had a clear and testable implication: if the effects we'd observed first with women and then with blacks were not entirely due to characteristics of these groups, but to stereotype and identity threat, as we argued, then similar effects should be observable in many groups, in relation to many different stereotypes, and in relation to many different performances and behaviors. Evidence showing this would add empirical heft to our emerging understanding. Back, then, to the through-line of this book, the expanding program of research on identity threat and its cures.

CHAPTER 5

The Many Experiences of Stereotype Threat

1.

When Ted McDougal, a white student at a prestigious university, walked into the first meeting of his African American political science class, he found himself counting. There were forty-five students in the class: one other, beside himself, was white; a few Asian students dotted the room; all the others were black. Ted didn't know much about African American experience. He had enrolled in the course to broaden himself. Yet, as he took his seat, he felt a question hanging over his head like a caption in a cartoon: What was this white guy doing in a class on African American politics?

The class began with history. It focused on the role of violence in maintaining whites' political dominance in the South after the

Civil War. Photographs of whippings were shown through PowerPoint. The professor pushed the students to put themselves in the shoes of the people involved in this drama. Discussion was vigorous. Ted noted that the black students started saying "we." He knew they weren't including him. Then the term "white people" emerged. "White people try to avoid this part of history." "White people don't want to take responsibility for these transgressions." He felt uncomfortable. He told me weeks later, in an interview we had as part of this research in a campus bookstore café, that he often worried about proving himself academically at this university. But in this class, he knew he had to prove himself in another way—as a good person, as an ally of the cause, as a nonracist white person.

In class, he felt he was multitasking. He was involved in the lectures and discussions, but he also worried that perhaps his statements, even his thoughts, would confirm the suspicion over his head. He kept his comments at the "tip of the iceberg" level, trying to be inoffensive—for example, saying out loud in class that he really liked the civil rights leader Bayard Rustin, while keeping to himself his ignorance about exactly what Rustin's role in the civil rights movement was. He was too reticent to pursue answers to his questions. He noticed the same thing in the other white student in class. Mostly, neither of them talked. Toward the end of that first day, as the professor went around the room asking the students to say their names and college major, he could hardly find his voice. His name came out more like "head" than "Ted." He sank in his seat.

Things hadn't gotten much better by the time our interview took place halfway through the quarter. I asked whether his tension interfered with his learning. He said he thought so. He described reading a section of St. Clair Drake and Horace Cayton's classic *Black Metropolis* in his dorm room. The section analyzed how a growing black population affected Chicago city politics in the mid-twentieth century. Ted said he hadn't been confident that he correctly understood the material. Maybe he was biased. Maybe his thinking was unknowingly contaminated by prejudice, stereotypes, or just naïveté. Even alone in his dorm room, his thinking was bottled up, insecure.

Yet he saw the class as positive for black students. "It gives them a chance to show how smart they are," he said. In most classes at his school, blacks are the minority, often a tiny minority. In those classes, they could feel the way he felt in this class. This is part of why he stayed in the class. Turnabout is fair play, but, most important, it was showing him something. He could see how the setting affected his "smartness." The pressure he felt confined his thought to the safe, the inoffensive, the superficial "tip of the iceberg." He hardly had one moment of unself-conscious engagement in the course's material. Yet he could see that the black students, whose experience and numbers enabled them to dominate the class, were unself-conscious, vigorously involved, and apt to say impressive things.

Our interview went on for a while. He had never expected the class to have so much of an effect on him. I explained the ideas my students and I were working on, about how the meaning of social identities like whiteness and blackness were rooted in situational contingencies. I said that was probably why he felt his "whiteness" so strongly in this class: it made him a minority there. Also, the topic of the class made negative stereotypes about whites—as racist or racially insensitive—constantly prominent. This put him under pressure, I explained.

I explained this pressure as a contingency of his identity in the class, his cross to bear. He listened. Encouraged, I became even more didactic, telling him he was probably learning something valuable. He was seeing into the experience of other groups, and that would give him the breadth he was after, make him more cosmopolitan. He listened. He said that would be nice. But as the interview closed, he said what impressed him most about the class was how it made him feel, how much it affected "smartness," his own and that of his black classmates.

Ted's experience in this class—his lack of participation, his self-consciousness, his hesitancy in thinking about the material, his lower-than-usual performance—would seem to reflect a threat similar to that experienced by women taking a difficult math test, or by blacks taking a difficult academic test of any sort. These threats differ as to form. The group identity involved is different. Ted is a white male, not a woman or a black. The aspect of his behavior affected by this threat was different; Ted was concerned about his lack of participation and self-consciousness in class more than about his performance per se. And the stereotype he worried about confirming was different: he was concerned about being seen as racially insensitive, not as unintelligent. He also knew that he was safe from this pressure in other classes where he was not a minority—unlike the blacks in this class, for whom this class was one of the few places they enjoyed such safety in numbers. Nonetheless, he experienced a stereotype threat in this class that affected him powerfully.

Ted's story makes a straightforward point: identity threat of the sort that has been shown to affect the intellectual performance of women and blacks is likely a general phenomenon that, in some form or another, in some situation or another, can affect anyone. There exists no group on earth that is not negatively stereotyped in some way—the old, the young, northerners, southerners, WASPs, computer whiz kids, Californians, and so forth. And when people with these identities are doing something, or are in a situation for which a negative stereotype about their group is relevant, they can feel stereotype threat; they can feel under pressure not to confirm the stereotype for fear that they will be judged or treated in terms of it. Identity threats like this—contingencies of identity—are part of everyone's life.

Yet early in our research we had no evidence that this was so, that identity threats are part of everyone's life. We'd shown its effect among strong women math students and among strong African American students. This was some generality: it happened in two groups, not just one. But a skeptic might argue that these two groups, women and blacks, had perhaps internalized the negative stereotype about their group's ability, and perhaps that internalization gave them a susceptibility to stereotype threat, a susceptibility necessary to get the effects we'd gotten in our experiments. Remember the Gordon Allport quote from chapter 3, "One's reputation, false or true, can't be hammered, hammered, hammered into one's head without doing something to one's character." Would someone show these effects if he hadn't grown up with this "hammering," and the self-doubt that Allport believes follows it?

As one often says in the science business, this is an "empirical question," a question that can be answered by research and therefore should be answered by research, not by speculation. Answering this question, we came to see, would take two steps. The first was to determine whether stereotype threat effects indeed required some prior susceptibility to the stereotype. The second was to see whether stereotype threat effects could actually be found in other groups—in reaction to different stereotypes and involving different behaviors.

We began with the first question, stewing about it in our lab group and with colleagues. At the time my colleague Lee Ross's office was across the hall from mine. Capable of seeing a problem from many sides, Lee is often referred to as a social psychologist's his once introduced him as the Charlie Parker of social psychology. He talks fast—he blows lots of notes with intricate themes, like the jazz saxophonist. You could do a lot worse than take an idea by his office to see what he thought. We talked.

An approach to our problem emerged. We'd have to do what seemed like the impossible: impose stereotype threat on a group in an area of performance where they weren't negatively stereotyped, and thus couldn't have an internalized stereotype susceptibility. If they then underperformed, we'd know that no prior susceptibility to the stereotype was necessary for them to experience this threat. We'd know that stereotype threat in the immediate situation was enough. If they didn't underperform, we would know that a prior susceptibility *was* necessary for them to experience this threat. But how to do this? How could we get a group to experience stereotype threat in an area where they weren't negatively stereotyped?

Joshua Aronson, Michael Lustina, Kelli Keough, Joseph Brown, Catherine Good, and I put our heads together and eventually came up with a strategy. We would put high-performing, highly confident white male math students under the stereotype threat of another group's—Asian Americans'—positive stereotype in math. We would tell them, just as they began a difficult math test that this was a study exploring Asians' strength in math and that the test they were taking was "one on which Asians tend to do better than whites." This would put them in a situation comparable to the one that women and blacks faced in the stereotype threat groups of our earlier experiments. They would be at risk of confirming their own group's math inferiority—this time not directly, but in relation to another group's stereotyped superiority. Their normal frustration on the test, then, could mean that, as whites, they had limited math ability relative to Asians. For white students who care about math, this perception, and the possibility of being judged or treated in terms of it, could be upsetting enough to distract them and undermine their test performance.

Yet white males have not lived with a stereotype about their group's math inferiority being "hammered into their heads" and should not, therefore, have the internalized self-doubts that such an experience could produce—and that could be a necessary component of the stereotype threat effects we'd observed with women and blacks. So if they underperformed after exposure to the Asian stereotype, we'd know that it was due to the situational impact of stereotype threat and not self-doubts acquired over a long socialization process.

That was our reasoning. Still, we knew it could be argued that white male math students, while not having their group's math inferiority directly "hammered into their heads," might still know the Asian-math stereotype and might have developed some sense of math inferiority relative to Asians. Several considerations told us not to worry too much about this. Knowing that another group is positively stereotyped in an activity doesn't imply that you are inferior because you're not a member of the group. Also, unless you've been close to a sizable population of strong Asian math students, you might not know about, or strongly believe, this stereotype.

Still, as a further precaution, we used only very strong white male math students in this study—Stanford students whose average score on the math SAT was 712 (on the 800-point scale for this test) and whose average self-rating of their math skills was very strong. It didn't seem likely that members of this group would have stereotype-based doubts about their math ability. So if they underperformed after exposure to the positive Asian stereotype, we could say with considerable confidence that it was due to the situational pressure of this indirect form of stereotype threat.

And this is just what happened. The results were dramatic. White males taking the difficult eighteen-item test, represented as one on which "Asians tend to do better than whites" performed, on average, a full three items worse than white male participants who were told nothing about the test.

The stereotype threat created by this comment impaired the math performance of *exceptionally strong white male* math students. No special self-doubting susceptibility seemed necessary.

At about this time, a different research team, all the way across the country at Harvard University, produced further evidence of the situational nature of stereotype threat—dramatic evidence at that. Margaret Shih, Todd L. Pittinsky, and Nalini Ambady asked the interesting question of how stereotype threat would work for a group of people who had two social identities relevant to a given performance domain, especially if one identity was positively stereotyped in the domain and the other identity was negatively stereotyped in the domain. They had in mind the case of Asian women performing math. Members of this group have two math-relevant identities: their gender identity, which is negatively stereotyped in math, and their ethnic identity, which is positively stereotyped in math.

If stereotype threat is largely a situational pressure, then it might be possible to change the math performance of Asian women, depending on which one of their performance-relevant identities they are reminded of in the situation—their ethnicity or their gender.

Shih and her colleagues asked undergraduate Asian women from Boston area colleges to participate in a study that had only two parts. They first filled out a brief background questionnaire and then took a difficult twenty-minute math test made up of twelve items from the Canadian Math Competition, a prestigious high school competition in Canada. The questions on the background questionnaire were used to remind the women of one or another of their math-relevant identities just before they took the test.

What the researchers found was clear. Women whose background questionnaire reminded them of their gender identity—with questions about whether their dorm was coed and why they would prefer coed living—got 43 percent of the math test questions they attempted correct, whereas women whose background questionnaire asked questions that did not remind them of their gender identity—with questions about their telephone service—got 49 percent of the questions they attempted correct. This comparison essentially replicated the detrimental effect of stereotype threat, among the gender-reminded women, on performance. Importantly, though, when the background questionnaire reminded them of their ethnic identity—with questions about what languages they spoke at home and how many generations of their family had lived in America—this underperformance was eliminated entirely. They got 54 percent of the items they attempted correct. Simply varying which of their identities they were reminded of before taking the twelve-item math test produced an average difference of two points in their score—an effect size that if played out over a typical, much longer test would depress overall performance dramatically.

These findings do not mean that math skills or even internalized math vulnerabilities—as internal traits of these women—had no effect on their performance. These internal characteristics may well have affected the general level of participants' performance. What they do show is that their math performance was further affected by which one of their identities was prominent in the test situation—the identity that exposes them to stereotype threat or the one that doesn't. This makes the important point that whatever the skills or vulnerabilities a group may have, situational differences in stereotype threat alone—a contingency of social identity—are fully sufficient to affect intellectual performance substantially.

And these findings suggest a possible remedy for stereotype threat effects: remind test takers of identities that counter the relevant stereotype. Some years earlier, a then graduate student Kirsten Stoutemeyer and I had inadvertently found evidence of this. Just before women math students took a difficult math test, we reminded them that they were Stanford students. This reminder greatly reduced stereotype threat's effect on their performance. We later found that R. B. McIntyre, R. M. Paulson, and Charles Lord had independently found the same thing. They dramatically reduced stereotype threat's impairment of women's math performance by reminding them, just before the test, of positive women role models.

Science, like life, is rarely definitive. But in light of the emerging results, we had confidence in a straightforward conclusion: stereotype threat isn't confined to particular groups, and if people have to have a susceptibility to experience it, that susceptibility doesn't have to be more than a simple familiarity with the relevant stereotype—and a commitment to doing well in that area of performance. As I described earlier, we also knew that stereotype threat affected the strongest students in the stereotyped group the most—another reason to doubt that self-doubt was a necessary component of one's susceptibility to stereotype threat. The picture was clearing up. Stereotype threat seemed to be a situational pressure that didn't require internal susceptibility to interfere with intellectual performance.

In order to know that this was so, we needed evidence of the breadth of stereotype threat effects. If no internal susceptibility was at the root of these effects, then it should be possible to observe them in a broad variety of groups and in relation to a broad variety of stereotypes. This was the task to which our lab and other social psychologists next turned.

2.

Jean-Claude Croizet is a French social psychologist with post-doctoral training in the United States. He is a man of medium height and, reflecting his penchant for marathon running, a thin build. He is curious and thoughtful, a careful thinker and careful researcher. He comes from the French working class in a society in which social class is as central a social division as race is in the United States. Perhaps this background led him to notice that something was undermining the intellectual and linguistic achievement of lower-class students at the French university where he taught, even the best prepared among them. As he considered how to study what he was seeing, he read the research that Josh Aronson and I had done, showing the effect of stereotype threat on African Americans' test performance.

His question to himself was essentially the generality question: Could the same thing that happened to strong African American students in our experiments be what was happening to lower-class French students in his classes? Could "stereotype threat"—the specific form it took for lower-class French students in French universities—be a cause of their language and performance troubles in college? Was stereotype threat a general part of the human experience?

Jean-Claude and his collaborator, Theresa Claire, gave this possibility its first test. They did an experiment at the University of Clermont-Ferrand, in southeastern France, with upper- and lower-class French college students that followed the experiment we had done at Stanford University with white and black Americans. They gave both groups, one at a time, a very difficult language test (again using GRE-type items). They told half of the participants that the test was diagnostic of language ability—an instruction that causes stereotype threat for the lower-class students by framing frustration on the test as confirmation of the French stereotype that lower-class people lack language ability. They told the other half of the participants that the test was nondiagnostic of ability, thus making the stereotype about social class and language ability irrelevant to their experience on the test.

The results mirrored those of my experiments with Josh exactly. When the twenty-one-item language test was said to be nondiagnostic of language ability, the lower-class French students performed slightly better than the upper-class French students, averaging 11.4 correct compared with an average of 10.3 correct for the upper-class French. But when the test was said to be diagnostic of language ability—thus making the stereotype about lower-class French students' ability relevant to their performance on this test— the lower-class French performed almost three items worse than the upper-class French. Stereotype threat—here stemming from stereotypes about language ability and social class rather than cognitive ability and race, or about math ability and sex—generalizes to a different group, in a different situation, in a different country and culture.

Back Stateside, Thomas Hess and his colleagues at North Carolina State University tested a generalization of stereotype threat that struck closer to home—that is, for a man of mellowing years like myself. There is, of course, a stereotype about aging and memory. Could the threat of confirming that stereotype actually affect memory among older people? To find out, one study asked older people (average age 70.8 years) and younger people (average age 19.3 years) to study some materials that included a memory test, a list of thirty words that participants studied for two minutes before trying to write down as many words on the list as they could remember. To make the stereotype about aging and memory vivid for some participants—thereby putting the older people in the group under the threat of confirming the stereotype—they had them first read a newspaper article claiming that age did, in fact, impair memory. Compared with participants who read no such article or who read an article claiming that age had little effect on memory, participants who read the stereotype-evoking article performed worse on the brief memory test, recalling 44 percent of the studied words compared with 58 percent by participants not under stereotype threat. In fact, in the group experiencing stereotype threat, the more aware the participants were of the aging stereotype, the worse they performed. And, as in so many stereotype threat experiments, the proportion of words recalled was worse for the older participants who cared most about having good memories.

As a last illustration of the emerging generality of stereotype threat effects, I remind you of the intriguing research by Jeff Stone and his colleagues at the University of Arizona, described in chapter 1, showing stereotype threat's effect on the golfing performance of athletically inclined Princeton students.

In the nearly fifteen years since its first demonstration was published, research on stereotype threat effects has blossomed throughout the world. The effect has been observed in women, African Americans, white males, Latino Americans, third-grade American schoolgirls, Asian American students, European males aspiring to be clinical psychologists (under the threat of negative stereotypes about men's ability to understand feelings), French college students, German grade school girls, U.S. soldiers on army bases in Italy, women business school students, white and black athletes, older Americans, and so on. It has been shown to affect many performances: math, verbal, analytic, and IQ test performance, golf putting, reaction time performance, language usage, aggressiveness in negotiations, memory performance, the height of athletic jumping, and so on. No special susceptibility is required to experience this pressure. Research has found but one prerequisite: the person must care about the performance in question. That's what makes the prospect of confirming the negative stereotype upsetting enough to interfere with that performance.

After I make this point in my talks, people often have several questions at once: What exactly does this threat do to a person that causes the interfering effects it has? What can be done to reduce the unwanted effects of stereotype threat in society and in their lives? And perhaps reflecting a certain frustration, they ask, Dear Professor, why can't a person just buckle down and overcome the damn stereotype? I can hear my parents' admonitions to this effect ringing in my ears as I write this. Future sections of the book will deal extensively with the first two questions. But now, sensing that frustration, I will address my parents' view, one shared by many—*I hear you, son, stereotype threat can be pretty bad, but you should use it to motivate you; get out there and prove the stereotype, and those who hold it, wrong.*

CHAPTER 6

Identity Threat and the Efforting Life

1.

Philip Uri Treisman is a mathematician who has created innovative workshops for teaching college math to students from groups whose math abilities are negatively stereotyped—first to black students at the University of California at Berkeley and then to women students at the University of Texas at Austin. Listening to him speak, one has the sense that he, like many mathematicians, learned the pleasure of mind work early in life. He pursues the interesting insight, the idea on which other ideas hinge.

His workshops are that kind of idea, one that earned him a MacArthur "genius" award early in his career. They rely on immersion in challenging math and, perhaps above all, on studying in groups—a technique that his success has helped to disseminate throughout the nation. Black students in his early workshops at Berkeley, for example, outperformed all other groups in their first-year calculus courses. A substantial portion of all of the American women who have gone on to study math at the graduate level in the United States come from Treisman's math workshops at the University of Texas.

But here I want to stress another part of his work: the essentially anthropological study he did early in his career, the study from which the idea for his workshops came. It began with an observation he made in the first-year calculus course he taught at Berkeley; it was the same observation I was to make later on when I visited the University of Michigan and saw grades of black and white students broken down by their entering SAT scores: black students were underperforming. In his first-year calculus course, among students who had similar math SATs when they entered Berkeley, black students regularly got lower grades than white and Asian students. I have always thought that one of Treisman's major insights was understanding that this situation didn't have to be accepted as normal. This is where his anthropology began.

With their permission, he began to literally follow his students around to observe them in their lives outside of class. He observed how, where, and with whom they studied. He spent time in their dorm rooms, followed them to the library. He hung out with them.

Soon a group difference came into view, one in which blacks and Asians differed the most, with whites in the middle. Asian students studied in groups, formal and informal, more than black and white students. This practice produced powerful advantages for learning calculus. It brought many heads to the homework, so that if one person couldn't solve a problem, someone else could, and that person could explain it. They could spend more time on the concepts involved in calculus, and less time doing the arithmetic of the homework. (It shortened homework time.) Misunderstandings could be quickly identified and corrected, even when they came from the teaching staff. Asian students also made little distinction between their academic and social lives. Saturday night studying in the library counted as social life for a group of friends bonded, in part, over studying and doing math problems together.

White students studied more independently. But they readily sought help from other students and teaching assistants. They talked shop about calculus outside of class, even compared notes on difficult problems, but focused their social lives less on academics than did Asian students.

Black students, Treisman found, offered a contrast to both styles. They were intensely independent, downright private about their work. After class, they returned to their rooms, closed the door and pushed through long hours of study—more hours than either whites or Asians. Many of them were the first of their family to attend college; they carried their family's hopes. What Treisman saw, sitting on the bunk bed, watching many of his black students work, explained a lot about what was happening to them in his class. With no one to talk to, the only way to tell whether they understood the concept of a problem was to check their answer in the back of the book. They spent considerable time doing this, which made them focus less on calculus concepts and more on rechecking their arithmetic against answers in the book. This tactic weakened their grasp of the concepts. Despite great effort, they often performed worse on classroom tests than whites and Asians, who they knew had studied no more, or even less, than they had. In light of the racial stereotype in the air over their heads, this was a frustrating experience, which made them wonder whether they belonged there.

Discouraged in this way, they didn't talk much academic shop outside of class, sternly separating their academic and social lives.

This, in turn, prevented them from knowing that other students, too, had anxieties and difficulties with their work; it allowed them to think that their problems were theirs exclusively, reflective of their own, or perhaps their group's, inability. As bad, it kept them from seeking help from the teaching staff. After a poor performance, they would redouble their efforts, but in the same isolated way. Intense work would be followed by relatively poor performance. Eventually they'd get discouraged, deciding that calculus and perhaps even Berkeley itself, wasn't for them. Also, having a lower grade in a gateway course like calculus made certain life aspirations less possible to achieve—being a physician, a dentist, or an engineer, for example. Already toward the end of their freshman course in calculus, these students, who had entered Berkeley with the highest aspirations just months earlier, were beginning to contract their goals. They'd give up trying to become a doctor. They'd try becoming a public health worker instead; that wouldn't require calculus.

Jeff was one of the students Treisman interviewed. He'd come to Berkeley from one of the best parochial high schools in San Francisco. His math SAT was close to 600, putting him in a high national percentile, especially for African American students. He was strongly motivated and came from a supportive family and community. Here is Treisman's description of his freshman year experience:

> In our first meeting, Jeff described to me with barely contained anger two white students who sat next to him during a calculus lecture reading Playboy and drinking beer from bottles they had concealed in a paper bag. Before the class midterm, he likened their behavior to blasphemy and predicted with evangelical fervor that "Justice will surely prevail." When he learned, several weeks later, that these white students received A's and he a C– on the

test, he was devastated. Shaken, Jeff went to see his teaching assistant as much to apologize for his poor performance as to seek help. The TA was quick to suggest that Jeff was not adequately prepared for the university and that he should consider transferring to a community college. Jeff withdrew from Berkeley at the end of his first term and, taking his TA's advice, enrolled at San Francisco City College the following semester.

Several years later, when we spoke again about his experience at the university, Jeff described the success of the beer-drinking students as "only the first blow." The final blow came when he received his first-term grades. He had not even predicted correctly which courses he would fail. Jeff's Subject A (remedial English) instructor, for example, had been so encouraging, so giving of her time: he could not understand how she could have failed him. He felt betrayed. He felt as if he were wandering in a maze. He could neither tell what was important in his courses, nor what he might do to improve his performance were he to try again. In addition to academic problems, Jeff had had a string of misunderstandings with administrative personnel in several campus offices. It seemed to him that these individuals were continually reneging on promises to him. He came to feel that he did not belong at the university.

Of course, things like this happen to other college students, too, regardless of their group identities. The very commonness of contracted aspirations early in college life makes it difficult to see a group pattern. As I've said, Treisman's insight was noticing this pattern and then going behind the scenes to understand it. There he saw black students—in an effort to succeed where their abilities are negatively stereotyped—following a strategy of intense, isolated effort, a strategy that often set them up for defeats and discouragements. They were trying hard, they were taking my father's advice (and probably their own father's advice), but they were trying to do it all by themselves, in a class where other people were working more happily and efficiently together, pooling their intellectual resources.

2.

My own suspicion that "over-efforting," if I can call it that, among the black students that Treisman had observed might be a general phenomenon, a broad fact of life, was strengthened by a conversation I had with a good friend, Carol Porter, on a visit some years ago to Princeton University.

Carol is a social psychologist who has devoted much of her career to bettering the undergraduate experience at universities like Princeton and Stanford. On the occasion in question, she and her dean had invited me to Princeton to consult about minority student life there. As the visit came to an end, Carol rather offhandedly told me about something she and others had seen while advising students about organic chemistry. This course is a national gateway to medical school; doing badly in it can derail your chances of getting in. It's also difficult, so Princeton students have developed strategies for getting through it. Some students sit through it one entire time before taking the course a second time for a grade. Others take the course during the summer at a presumably less competitive school and then try to have the credit for it transferred back to Princeton. When advisers see students having difficulty in this course, they might suggest one of these strategies so that the students don't stay in the course, get a bad grade, and undermine their chances for medical school.

Carol said that when this advice is offered to white and Asian students, most of them readily take it, dropping the course for a grade and following one of the alternate strategies. To Carol's surprise, though, when the advice is offered to black students having trouble, they more often rejected it, persisting in the course past the point when one can drop it without getting a grade, and thus often getting a low grade that jeopardized their medical school chances.

By this time, I knew about Treisman's research. What Carol was telling me seemed like another expression of what he had observed. It was as if the black students she described were staying in this course to disprove the stereotype hanging over their heads—following their and my parents' advice. They pushed on when a person not facing this "allegation" might have simply switched to a better strategy. Over-effort at Princeton, too?

"Over-efforting" had now popped up in several achievement contexts, enough to suggest that under some circumstances it might cause academic underperformance. Or so David Nussbaum and I thought as we surveyed these instances. David was a new graduate student who had been a philosophy major as an undergraduate at Yale. He loves to, as they say in philosophy, "parse" questions, closely analyzing their meaning and logic. We faced an interesting question worth parsing: Was the syndrome of over-effort and self-sufficiency evidenced in Treisman's research, and the observations of Carol Porter's organic chemistry advisers, caused by stereotype and identity threat? Or was it perhaps a general characteristic of African Americans that stems from a socialization process—again, I hear my own father's words in my ears—that stresses working twice as hard as others to succeed? Perhaps that advice gets internalized as a principle of conduct and fosters intense effort even in situations that pose no identity threat.

As I said, David is a good parser of questions, and this led to a simple experiment with two aims. The first was to see whether the over-efforting syndrome could be evoked in a laboratory experiment; the second was to test, if it could be evoked, which of these two understandings of it was the more accurate.

We focused the experiment on the solution of anagrams, a task that involves rearranging sets of scrambled letters into meaningful words. Anagrams can be very easy to solve, as in "ebd" being easily rearranged into "bed," or very difficult to solve, as in "ferhziidsaenncd" being rearranged into "disenfranchised." In the first part of the experiment, we gave black and white Stanford students twenty very difficult anagrams to solve. We wanted the task to be hard and frustrating, something on which they knew they hadn't done well, something like a calculus or an organic chemistry class perhaps. A second problem-solving task was to include both anagrams and analogy problems. We asked them to pick as many anagram problems to include on this second task as they wanted to. This measured how much our participants wanted to continue trying to solve the kind of anagrams they had just had trouble with on the first task—this being analogous to how much students having trouble with organic chemistry might want to stay in the course and risk failure. We got a straightforward answer: they didn't want to do very many. When the anagram task was presented as just a laboratory task, neither black nor white participants agreed to do many more of them—a polite four or five at the most. When it was just a laboratory task, there was no over-efforting on the part of any participants. They were able to stop doing the difficult anagrams the way white and Asian students had been able to stop and reschedule a frustrating organic chemistry class.

Another group of participants, however, went through exactly the same procedure, except that they were told the anagram task was a measure of cognitive abilities. For the black students in this group, this labeling made the stereotype about blacks' cognitive abilities relevant to the anagram task. Their frustration on the task could now confirm the stereotype about their group's abilities. Unlike the whites in this group, then, they were now under stereotype threat.

How would they now respond to the invitation to do more anagrams on the second task? Would they do fewer to perhaps avoid stereotype threat? Or, as students identified with their cognitive abilities, would they follow my father's advice and do more to try to disprove the stereotype? Again, we got a clear answer. They behaved just like the black students Treisman had observed in the Berkeley dorm rooms, and just like the students Carol Porter had described in Princeton's organic chemistry course. They persisted, big-time. White participants in this group, being under no stereotype threat, agreed to do the same polite four additional anagrams that participants in the no stereotype threat groups had agreed to do. Black students in this group, however, agreed to do a whopping eight additional anagrams, twice as many—over-efforting to the max.

We thus had answers to both of our questions. Academic over-efforting among black students could be evoked in the laboratory—easily so. It's a real phenomenon. Second, it seems to be caused by the identity pressure of stereotype threat. It didn't happen without this threat, when the anagrams were presented as just anagrams, as puzzles unrelated to cognitive abilities. Black participants weren't just supermotivated students. When they weren't under stereotype threat, they didn't try any harder than anyone else. But when there was a stereotype to disprove, they tried twice as hard as everyone else—expending precisely the amount of extra effort that my father's classic piece of advice specifies.

If these black students had academic troubles, they wouldn't seem to have come from a tendency to give up in the face of frustration and stereotype pressure. They tried extremely hard in the face of pressure, like their counterparts in the organic chemistry

and calculus courses I described. They didn't need parental prod-
ding. When the stereotype about their group's abilities was in play,
they tried extra hard on their own.

3.

So is this extra motivation always a problem for performance and
achievement? Could literally millions of parents all be wrong? In
the African American community, Jackie Robinson's story is legendary. *Ebony* magazine has run a page every month for over fifty
years featuring people who have broken down one racial barrier or
another. Using the motivation to overcome barriers and stereotypes
to fuel achievement is a central theme of black life in America, as it
is for other groups contending with negative stereotypes—women,
for example. Does this motive always backfire when it comes to
performance and achievement?

Most of the stereotype threat research has focused on difficult
work at the frontier of a person's skills—demanding math tests, IQ
tests that get progressively more challenging, verbal tests pitched
to the limit of one's skills, rigorous college curricula, and so on.
Frustration on these tasks makes the stereotype personally relevant
as a plausible explanation for why they are having the frustration.
It threatens them with the fear of confirming the negative stereotype, which causes distracting emotion and thoughts. Performance
gets worse. The risk of confirming the stereotype gets worse. A
vicious cycle ensues. This is how the extra motive to disprove the
stereotype seems to interfere with performance at the frontier of
one's skills—in organic chemistry, for example. (The next chapter
examines these processes more closely.)

But what happens when you perform easily and well in a
domain where your group is negatively stereotyped—that is, what

happens when the task is well enough within your skill level that you don't experience much frustration in doing it? A performance like that is essentially a refutation of the stereotype, and since it's a refutation, and since you can do it pretty easily, you might imagine being especially motivated to perform well. In that kind of situation, the stereotype-disproving motive might produce better performance.

Two social psychologists at the University of Kansas, Laurie O'Brien and Christian Crandall, had independently decided to test this exact idea and came up with a straightforward experiment to do it. They gave a sample of men and women students at the University of Kansas one difficult and one easier math test. The easier test asked them to do as many three-digit multiplications as they could in a ten-minute period. The difficult test asked them to do fifteen algebra problems from the math section of the SAT in the same period. One group took the tests under stereotype threat. Participants were told the tests had previously shown gender differences. The other group took the tests under no stereotype threat. Its participants were told that these particular tests did not show gender differences. What happened supported O'Brien and Crandall's reasoning. On the difficult test, women did worse under stereotype threat than women not under stereotype threat and worse than men in either group. But the tables were turned on the easier test. *Women under stereotype threat did better than women under no stereotype threat and better than men in either group.*

At the frontier of their skills, stereotype threat and the motive to disprove the stereotype hurt performance, presumably through the set of interfering reactions described earlier. But back a ways from that frontier, where the task was easier and the frustration less intense, trying to disprove the stereotype boosted performance beyond that of all other groups.

Here was a point for the parents. Presumably, it was seeing

something like this that convinced my father and millions of other parents that the drive to defeat stereotypes could be harnessed for achievement. It can be. The O'Brien and Crandall experiment shows that when the work is manageable, an extra motivation to disprove a stereotype can raise performance to a level higher than it would otherwise reach.

What does this motive to "disprove" the stereotype look like in real life? Does it turn people into superachievers and workaholics? Valerie Jones, a creative graduate student in my lab with a penchant for doing research in real-life situations, and I did a simple survey to shed light on this question. The idea was this: in workplaces where women are numerically underrepresented, they might experience more pressure to prove themselves by working hard and disproving negative stereotypes than in workplaces where women are less underrepresented. Valerie surveyed forty-one women attending a local Silicon Valley conference on women in technology. She asked them questions about the number of women in their workplace and about how much pressure they felt to prove themselves by working harder. The results were very suggestive. Compared with women from the less underrepresented settings, women from the more underrepresented settings reported feeling substantially more pressure to prove themselves through work and reported more behaviors that reflected this pressure, like getting to work earlier, leaving later, and engaging in fewer activities outside of work. In real life too, then, there is evidence that women can use the stereotype-driven pressure to prove themselves as a motive for good—or at least as a motive to work harder.

But is this an unalloyed good? When all of these research findings are taken together, one might have to say perhaps not. The problem is that the pressure to disprove a stereotype changes what you are *about* in a situation. It gives you an additional task. In addition to learning new skills, knowledge, and ways of thinking in a schooling situation, or in addition to trying to perform well in a workplace like the women in the high-tech firms, you are also trying to slay a ghost in the room, the negative stereotype and its allegation about you and your group. You are multitasking, and because the stakes involved are high—survival and success versus failure in an area that is important to you—this multitasking is stressful and distracting.

It has major consequences. First, the stress and distraction it causes (as we shall see in more detail in the next chapter) can directly interfere with performance, especially when what you are doing is at the limits of your skills and knowledge—precisely where you need to be working in order to learn and develop. Also, as we can see from Jeff's story and Treisman's observations, it can cause highly inefficient strategies and rigidities. You are not just learning or performing; you are also refuting a stereotype. So you can't just drop organic chemistry for credit and plan to retake it the next semester. That could feel as if you were confirming the stereotype, as a characterization of yourself and of your group. You have to hang in there, even if it costs you your preferred career path.

And when you realize that this stressful experience is probably a chronic feature of the setting for you, it can be difficult for you to stay in the setting, to sustain your motivation to succeed there. Disproving a stereotype is a Sisyphean task; something you have to do over and over again as long as you are in the domain where the stereotype applies. Jeff seemed to feel this way about Berkeley, that he couldn't find a place there where he could be seen as belonging. When men drop out of quantitative majors in college, it is usually because they have bad grades. But when women drop out of quantitative majors in college it usually has nothing to do with their grades. The culprit, in their case, is not their quantitative skills but, more likely, the prospect of living a significant portion of their lives in a domain where they may forever have to prove themselves—and with the chronic stress that goes with that.

This is not an argument against trying hard, or against choosing the stressful path. There is no development without effort; and there is seldom great achievement, or boundary breaking, without stress. And to the benefit of us all, many people have stood up to these pressures. (We will read about some in the next chapter.) The focus here, instead, is on what has to be gotten out of the way to make these playing fields more level. People experiencing stereotype threat are already trying hard. They're identified with their performance. They have motivation. It's the extra ghost slaying that is in their way.

There is a syndrome here, one that my father, I, and many other parents may not have fully appreciated. Under limited circumstances, the motivation to disprove stereotypes can have constructive effects. But at precisely the point where performance and ease of functioning are most important—at the limits of one's skills and knowledge as one tries to develop and grow at school and work—this form of motivation very often backfires. There, ironically, it can cause the very group underperformance that so many parents had hoped to coach their children around.

Chapter 9 will take up solutions to this problem, things that individuals and institutions alike can do to reduce this pressure and the underperformance it causes. But it's important not to leave this chapter without noting that Treisman found a solution to Jeff's problem that worked dramatically well, and that thereby both reinforces the analysis emerging here and shows that cures derived from it can be effective and feasible.

He conceived a program that, as far as studying calculus is concerned, and put a bit crudely, tried to get black students to study more like Asian students—in particular, to work in groups, groups that spent a lot of time (at least six hours per week) together outside of class talking about calculus, among other things. He expected the same advantages he'd observed in the Asian groups: with multiple people studying the problems together, they could spend proportionately more time learning critical concepts and less time doing answer-checking arithmetic; they could more accurately gauge their understanding and proficiency; they could be more certain about interactions with the teaching staff; and so on. It worked. They got better grades; the black students in Treisman's workshop now earned better first-year calculus grades than either the white or Asian students in the regular calculus classes at Berkeley. If only Treisman had developed these in time to help Jeff.

Treisman's workshops teach the skills of group learning that directly make learning calculus easier. But what were these skills correcting for? Here his anthropological research was revealing. They were correcting a tendency among these black students to protectively isolate themselves and to over commit to self-sufficiency—strategies that might help them avoid people who they worried might stereotype them, but that would also isolate them from help they needed. It wasn't that these students lacked parental advice. It was following that advice to distraction that was the problem. Nor was getting them to care about their work. What Treisman solved was how they could better implement the caring they already had.

In recent years, a number of ingenious scientists have begun to uncover precisely what this predicament of identity does to a person, and precisely how the things it does to a person cause the performance and persistence problems that launched this research. It's in seeing these effects that I believe one finally sees the power of this predicament and why, for example, it makes my father's advice—necessary though it may be—insufficient.

CHAPTER 7

The Mind on Stereotype Threat: Racing and Overloaded

1.

Some years ago Donald Dutton and Arthur Aron, two social psychologists, asked a group of male college students to walk, one at a time, across the Capilano Bridge just outside of Vancouver, British Columbia, in Canada. The Capilano Bridge is a narrow, wobbly walkway with a rope handrail 450 feet long that spans the Capilano River, 230 feet below. As each man reached the other side, he was met by an attractive young woman interviewer who, after getting him to complete a questionnaire, gave him her phone number and invited him to call her if he had any further questions about the study she was ostensibly doing.

Dutton and Aron were interested in a basic question about human nature: Do we have direct knowledge of our emotions, or can we be so out of touch with them that sometimes we are unaware of them or get them confused, mistaking one emotion for another?

This big question about human nature was boiled down, in their experiment, to a concrete question: Could the lingering anxiety that these men had after they crossed the Capilano Bridge be mistaken by them as attraction for the young woman interviewer they met on the other side? If we don't always have direct knowledge of our emotions, and if one emotion can sometimes be mistaken for another, then these men might mistake the dissipating anxiety they experienced after crossing the scary bridge as attraction for the young woman now standing right in front of them. Dutton and Aron measured attraction toward the young woman as the number of men who called her that night for "additional information."

Two other groups participated in the experiment. In one, men crossed the Capilano Bridge, but met a male interviewer on the other side. This group tested whether the lingering anxiety from the bridge crossing could somehow cause more phone calls, even when it didn't—in all likelihood—make the interviewer more attractive. In the last group, men met the attractive woman interviewer, but they didn't cross the Capilano Bridge, they crossed a bridge that was solid and low to the ground, a bridge crossing that caused no anxiety. This group tested whether the attractiveness of the interviewer was able, by itself, to inspire more telephone calls that night.

What happened? Many more of the men who met the young woman after crossing the Capilano Bridge called her that night than did men in either of the other two groups. Crossing this bridge had caused anxiety, which had lingered for a while. Not having direct awareness of this anxiety, and then being face to face with an attractive young woman, these men interpreted their feelings not as anxiety, but as intense attraction.

Men in the other groups could apparently keep things straight. When the interviewer was male, they didn't mistake their lingering anxiety for attraction. There was simply no cue in that situation that could make attraction seem like a plausible emotion to be having. And for the men who crossed an unscary bridge, there was simply no lingering anxiety to fuel any special attraction for the interviewer. Men in these groups seldom called.

Our ability to grasp our emotions, then, is not perfect. When they are very strong, it is easier to know them directly. But when they are moderate, like the lingering anxiety one would feel after crossing the Capilano Bridge, we have less direct access to them. To know and interpret our more moderate emotions, we rely more on what's going on in the immediate situation. Standing in front of the attractive interviewer, the men in the Dutton and Aron experiment who had just crossed the Capilano Bridge felt an intense attraction, even though what fueled that attraction was lingering anxiety from having crossed a scary bridge.

2.

It's a good thing Steve Spencer, Josh Aronson, and I knew this when we turned to the problem of *how* identity threat has its effects, because we ran smack into this limitation of human functioning, people's limited access to their feelings and to the causes of their feelings. We had always assumed that identity threat made people anxious and that it was the anxiety it caused that directly impaired performance. Anxiety, we thought, was the performance-damaging handmaiden of threat. It seemed obvious.

In our very first experiments, though, when Steve and I asked women taking a difficult math test under stereotype threat how anxious they felt, they reported no more anxiety than women taking the test under no stereotype threat (that is, when they understood the test to show no gender differences). The women performed worse under stereotype threat—the finding that launched this research—but they didn't report being any more anxious. We were puzzled.

Later on, Josh and I got further puzzling results. As the data came in showing the effects of stereotype threat on black students' verbal test performance, our feet on the desk, we wondered whether the threat was making them anxious and whether that was why they underperformed. Josh started interviewing our research participants. He found nothing: those under stereotype threat reported no more anxiety than those not under stereotype threat. The stereotype threat participants seemed calm, resolved. They said the test was difficult, but that they were determined to bear down and do well. They believed that their effort would see them through. They said these things even as we could see from their test booklets that they hadn't done well at all.

So it was a good thing that we knew how limited people are in reporting on internal states like anxiety. It helped us not be convinced by the lack of evidence showing anxiety reactions to stereotype threat. And it helped us take more seriously some of the counterevidence. Remember that people under stereotype threat completed more word fragments with words related to the stereotype. This suggests they were anxious about confirming the stereotype or being seen as confirming it. Black students under stereotype threat also did other things that suggested they were anxious about being stereotyped. They reported less preference for things associated with blacks—jazz, hip-hop, and basketball—and more preference for things associated with whites—classical music, tennis, and swimming. They offered more excuses in advance of their performance, like saying they got little sleep the night before. Such tendencies suggested they were anxious. But these same participants wouldn't directly tell us they were anxious. Perhaps they didn't want to admit to it. Or perhaps, like the men who met the attractive interviewer after crossing the Capilano Bridge, they didn't know they were anxious.

To know how central anxiety was to stereotype threat effects, we needed a better measure of anxiety, one that didn't depend on what people knew about themselves.

3.

Led by James Blascovich, of the University of California at Santa Barbara, a team—Steve Spencer, Dianne Quinn, and I—did an experiment that directly measured a physiological component of stress and anxiety, mean arterial blood pressure (MAP). The experiment was pretty much like any other stereotype threat experiment, except for a few differences. As black and white college students arrived at the laboratory, they were hooked up to cardiovascular recording equipment to ostensibly measure their physiological reactions to mental tasks. Five minutes later, after a baseline blood pressure had been collected, they began a verbal task—a version of what's called the Remote Association Task, each item of which gives three words that requires the participant to come up with a fourth word that relates to the given words, as in "cheese" relating to "mouse," "sharp," and "blue." They understood this task to be a test of intelligence.

Participants in the stereotype threat group were told nothing more. Remember, understanding the task as an intelligence test is all it takes to put blacks at risk of confirming the stereotype about their intellectual abilities.

For the no stereotype threat group, the test was said to be "race-fair." It was said that blacks always did as well as whites on this particular test, and that the test had been developed at black colleges by a racially integrated research team. These statements made the stereotype about black's ability implausible as an interpretation of their performance on this particular test.

The results were dramatic. The blood pressure of both the white and the black participants who were told the test was "race-fair" (under no stereotype threat) actually dropped from the time the blood pressure cuff was put on to the time they were in the middle of the test. The same was true for whites to whom the test was presented as an intelligence test. But the mean arterial blood pressure of their black counterparts rose dramatically while they took the test. People under stereotype threat might not be able to report that they were anxious or even whether their feelings were anxiety or love, but it didn't mean that they weren't anxious. Their physiological responses told us plainly they were.

Soon our understanding of stereotype threat's physiological effects broadened even more. Wendy Mendes—a longtime colleague of James Blascovich—and another team of researchers tested whether the stereotype threat that whites can feel interacting with blacks would elevate blood pressure. Their experiment was starkly simple. While hooked up to a blood pressure cuff, they had white college students simply talk to either a white or black fellow student whom they didn't know. Talking to a black stranger, compared with talking to a white stranger, should put white participants at greater risk of being seen stereotypically, as perhaps racially insensitive. And if this stereotype threat causes anxiety, these participants should have higher blood pressure. They did, substantially higher.

A picture was emerging. Even though people don't seem very consciously aware of it, an identity threat like stereotype threat is enough to cause anxiety as measured by blood pressure. But, you might ask, how much anxiety? Is the anxiety caused by identity threat strong enough to interfere with functioning, with a person's ability to perform tasks, for example?

Suppose I put a person under some form of stereotype threat— say, I had a group of women identified with math who expect to take a very difficult math test—and then I asked them to do something easy and something difficult, like repeatedly writing their names forward, the easy thing, and repeatedly writing their names backward, the difficult thing. Would the anxiety and arousal caused by this stereotype threat be enough to actually interfere with their performance of these tasks?

This is an interesting experiment because the handwriting tasks are unrelated to the math stereotype. Doing them badly would not confirm the stereotype about women's math ability. The fear of confirming this stereotype would not affect their performance on these tasks. The only thing that could affect their performance on these tasks would be the anxiety caused by the identity threat these women felt as they waited for the difficult math test. If that anxiety alone is enough to interfere with their performance, then these women shouldn't do very well on the handwriting tasks, perhaps especially not on the difficult task of writing their names backward.

This is the question that Avi Ben-Zeev and his students at San Francisco State University asked in an experiment they set up precisely this way. They obtained a clear answer. Even the modest anxiety that math-identified women experienced while waiting for a difficult math test—nothing like the arousal caused by crossing the Capilano Bridge or by taking a real-life, high-stakes SAT math test—was enough to interfere with how well they could write their name backward. Identity threat is a constant presence. The typical laboratory experiment can implement this threat, in good conscience, to only a modest degree—for example, the amount women experience waiting for a math test in an experiment versus the amount they would experience waiting for a real Graduate Record Exam. But even these limited implementations cause enough cardiovascular stress to make them stumble in doing even modestly difficult things.

So we can say now that part of stereotype threat's effect—its impairment of women's math performance, of lower-class French students' performance on language exams, of white males' miniature golf performance, and so on—is caused directly by its effect of increasing heart rate, blood pressure, and related physiological signs of anxiety to the point that these reactions interfere with performance. We can also say that people aren't much aware of this as it is happening. They don't report it when asked. It's a cost we don't seem to recognize we're paying. But is it the only way identity threat interferes with performance? Wouldn't it directly affect our thinking as well?

4.

As you will see, the answer is yes. It makes us worry about confirming the stereotype ("Will I be seen as in over my head?"), about the consequences of doing so ("How will people react if they think I'm racist?"), about what we have to do to beat the stereotype ("Will I have a chance to show these people that I am a good person?"), and so on. It induces rumination, which takes up mental capacity, distracting us from the task at hand—from the questions on the standardized test we're taking or from the conversation we're having with persons of a different race. So beyond the physiological reactions that identity threat causes, it also impairs performance and other actions by interfering with our thinking.

Or at least that is what Jean-Claude Croizet, the French social psychologist I introduced in chapter 5, and his colleagues thought.

They found a particularly ingenious way to test this idea. It hinged on a little-known but astonishingly simple piece of human physiology, a direct connection between mind and body: the intervals between your heartbeats tend to be more stable the more involved you are in mental activity, or the greater your "cognitive load," in psychology parlance. This phenomenon reflects the metabolic demands of mental activity, and it means that the variation in how fast your heart is beating is an indicator of how much you are thinking. The greater the cognitive load, the more stable your heartbeat interval; the less that load, the more variable this interval.

With this fact in mind, and the requisite physiological recording equipment in hand, Croizet and his group tested a simple idea: if stereotype threat imposes a greater cognitive load on people by pressuring them to ruminate about the threat and its consequences, then people under stereotype threat should have more-stable heartbeat intervals than people not under stereotype threat.

Croizet's team took advantage of what we psychologists find to be an especially unsavory stereotype at his French university: that science majors are smarter than psychology majors. We hate it. But there it is. The team gave science and psychology majors the Raven's Progressive Matrices IQ test and got a standard pattern of stereotype threat results. The psychology majors scored lower than the science majors when the test was represented as an IQ test—thus putting the psychology majors at risk of confirming the negative stereotype about their groups' intelligence—but they scored the same as science majors when this pressure was removed by representing the test as essentially a puzzle, nondiagnostic of intelligence.

Of course, Croizet and his colleagues were interested in something else. They measured heartbeat intervals throughout the IQ test for all participants. They found that the interval was more stable for all of those who thought it was an IQ test. Both psychology majors, who were under stereotype threat, and science majors, who were under less stereotype threat during this IQ test, seemed to be bearing a substantial cognitive load. It was something else that distinguished the two groups: the relationship between their heartbeat interval and how well they performed. The harder the science majors (under less stereotype threat) thought, as indicated by a more stable heartbeat interval, the better they did. But the harder the psychology majors (at risk of confirming the stereotype) thought, the more stable their heartbeat interval, the worse they did. Hard thinking for the science majors, under little stereotype pressure, reflected constructive engagement with the test. Hard thinking for the psychology majors, at risk of confirming the stereotype, reflected performance-worsening rumination.

When we're at risk of confirming a stereotype that we don't like, and it's about something we care about, our minds race. They're probably doing all sorts of things: arguing against the stereotype; denying its applicability to us; disparaging anyone who could ever think that of us; feeling sorry for ourselves; trying to buck ourselves up to disprove the stereotype. We are defending ourselves and coping with the threat of being stereotyped. We're probably aware of some of this defending and coping. But much of the time we may miss it, unless we try very hard to listen. A big implication of the Croizet team's finding is that a mind trying to defeat a stereotype leaves little mental capacity free for anything else we're doing.

Two psychologists from the University of Arizona, Toni Schmader and her then graduate student Michael Johns, developed a precise model of exactly what capacities the racing mind interferes with. Its core impairment is working memory, "the type of memory used to retain and manipulate information for immediate or near immediate use" (p. 44), such as for taking tests, participating in conversations or discussions, or reading homework assignments for an African American political science class all alone in a dorm room.

Schmader and Johns asked college women interested in math to count the vowels in a number of sentences, and between the sentences they inserted unrelated words. They found that women under the stereotype threat of waiting to take a difficult math test could count the vowels in the sentences just fine, but couldn't remember the words between the sentences—at least not as well as women who, because they were waiting to take a nondescript problem-solving test, were not under stereotype threat. The racing mind at work. It impaired the ability of women under stereotype threat to pick up the extra words between the sentences; that is, it impaired their working memory capacity. And just as important, Schmader and Johns showed that the more stereotype threat impaired this capacity—as shown by fewer incidental words being remembered—the worse the women performed on the subsequent math test. Stereotype threat's impairment of working memory directly caused its impairment of math performance.

Schmader and Johns developed a model of the racing mind. First, the threat of confirming the stereotype makes us vigilant to all things relevant to the threat, and to what our chances of avoiding it are. Second, it raises self-doubt and then rumination over how warranted the doubts are. Third, these concerns lead us to constantly monitor how well we're doing (something that can cause "choking" in athletes, for example). Finally, it pressures us to suppress threatening thoughts, thoughts about not doing well or about bad consequences of confirming the stereotype. Ever been there? If so, you know that that's a lot of mental activity, and while it's going on, there isn't much mind left over for other things.

This view is further corroborated by the research of Anne Krendl, Jennifer Richeson, William Kelley, and Todd Heatherton, who used fMRI imaging technology to examine stereotype threat's effect on brain activity. They invited twenty-eight strong women math students to solve fifty difficult math problems while lying in an fMRI brain scanner. By detecting blood flow in regions of the brain, the scanner could measure the level of mental activity in different brain regions as the women did the math. Half of the women were under stereotype threat while they worked (having been reminded that "research has shown gender differences in math ability and performance" before starting the math problems); the other half were not under stereotype threat, or were under relatively less of it while they worked (having not been reminded of the math gender stereotype).

What neural structures were activated by stereotype threat? They found a clear pattern: "Although women [not under stereotype threat] recruited neural networks that [from previous research] are associated with mathematical learning (i.e., angular gyrus, left parietal and prefrontal cortex), women who were [under stereotype threat] did not recruit these regions, and instead revealed heightened activation in a neural region [that from previous research is] associated with social and emotional processing (ventral anterior cingulate cortex)" (p. 168). Stereotype threat dampened down activity in the part of the brain we use to do mathematics and increased activity in the part of the brain associated with vigilance to one's social context and to emotion. Again, in the authors' words, "stereotype threat may direct women's attention toward the negative social and emotional consequences of confirming negative stereotypes about their group, thereby increasing performance anxiety" (p. 173). Other research teams have produced similar results, and research in this area is rapidly expanding our understanding of the neural structures affected by stereotype threat.

But even now, thanks to the physiological research, the research on cognitive load, the thinking of Schmader and Johns, and the brain research, a strong working consensus as to how stereotype threat affects us is emerging. It's this: stereotype and identity threats—these contingencies of identity—increase vigilance toward possible threat and bad consequences in the social environment, which diverts attention and mental capacity away from the task at hand, which worsens performance and general functioning, all of which further exacerbates anxiety, which further intensifies the vigilance for threat and the diversion of attention. A full-scale vicious cycle ensues, with great cost to performance and general functioning.

Something like this happened to Ted in his African American political science class. It happened to all of the participants under stereotype threat in all of the stereotype threat experiments. It often happens to ability-stereotyped people on real-life tests, when they talk to their teachers or when they participate in classrooms, labs, and workplaces where they could confirm the stereotypes they hate. Their minds race, their blood pressure rises, they begin to sweat, they redouble their efforts, they try to refute the stereotype in their own minds and what they can't refute they try to suppress, the brain activity that underlies vigilance to threat increases, and this further suppresses the brain activity critical to performance and functioning. When the work is difficult, the people often underperform. The more they care, the more frustrated they are, and the higher the stakes of performance, the more these things happen. And if the threat is part of an ongoing situation in their lives—part of their ongoing experience in a workplace, for example, in a college major, in a relationship, in a school—then these reactions can become ongoing, chronic contingencies of their identity.

And all the while, the persons may have no more conscious grasp of what's going on than the men who crossed the Capilano Bridge had of why they were so attracted to the woman interviewer.

There is, then, a clear set of facts on the ground. We know that stereotype threat has real effects on people. It causes a racing mind and a full complement of physiological and behavioral effects. We know that people aren't much aware of all this as it's happening, or at least they don't want to acknowledge it. We also know that these threats and their effects are identity threats and effects, which go with particular social identities in particular situations: women in advanced math, white males very likely in the last 10 meters of the 100-meter dash, blacks in the vanguard of their class, and so on.

These effects are important. But they have been studied primarily in single-episode experiments. Thus, I've gotten curious about what happens when these threats become chronic, when they are an ongoing experience in some area of one's life. People are in classrooms, workplaces, college majors, areas of sports, and the like, not just for a single episode but for long periods—months, years, sometimes decades. What happens then?

The facts suggest a worrisome answer: if people are under threats from stereotypes or other identity contingencies for long periods, they may pay a tax. The persistent extra pressure may undermine their sense of well-being and happiness, as well as contribute to health problems caused by prolonged exposure to the physiological effects of the threat. And all the while, like the participants in the Capilano Bridge study, they may have little awareness that they are paying this tax.

This thinking led me to ask a simple question: Is there any evidence of what long-term exposure to identity threats does to people?

5.

Enter a soft-spoken, intellectually precise African American epidemiologist and public health researcher named Sherman James. Born and raised in Hartsville, South Carolina, James majored in psychology at Talladega College and got a Ph.D. in psychology from Washington University in St. Louis, Missouri. Toward the end of graduate school an old high school friend told James about his work in epidemiology and environmental health. James was impressed. It was what he had always wanted to do. A year passed. Then, while finishing his graduate training, apparently out of the blue, he got a call from the chair of the epidemiology department at the University of North Carolina Medical School in Chapel Hill. He was being offered a job; an assistant professorship in epidemiology. He couldn't explain why he'd gotten the call, but he knew what to say: yes.

At North Carolina, he threw himself into the issue of racial disparities in health. This brought him to a well-known phenomenon: black Americans, both men and women, have higher rates of hypertension (blood pressure above 140/90) than white Americans. A recent report stated, "[N]early a third of black men (34%) and black women (31%) are considered hypertensive, compared to 25% and 21% of white men and women, respectively." One might think these disparities are due, in part, to black-white differences in income, education level, body mass index, smoking, and the like, all factors that cause hypertension. But these disparities persist even when they are adjusted for the effect of these factors. One might think the genetics of African ancestry contribute, but black Africans don't show elevated blood pressure.

James took up the mystery. He began writing a research grant. His preparation included interviewing black hypertensive outpatients at the University of North Carolina Hospital. One man was especially memorable, a raconteur and local community leader who regaled James with stories of his life triumphs.

The man was born in the upper Piedmont area of North Carolina in 1907 into the extreme poverty of a sharecropping family. Although he eventually learned to read and write, he went to school only through the second grade. But as James writes,

Even more impressive . . . through unrelenting hard work and determination . . . against tremendous odds—he freed himself and his offspring from the debt of bondage of the sharecropper system. Specifically, by the time he was 40 years of age, he owned 75 acres of fertile North Carolina farmland. . . . [But] by his late 50's, he suffered from hypertension, arthritis, and a case of peptic ulcer disease so severe that 40% of his stomach had to be removed. (p. 167)

One day James visited the man for a noon interview. They sat in the backyard. The man began his stories of struggle and triumph. After a while, his wife yelled from the house, "John Henry . . . it's time for lunch." Listening to the man's efforts in the face of hardship, and then hearing his name, gave James an idea that would shape the rest of his career. The man's name was the same as that of the legendary John Henry, the "steel drivin'" man of American folklore, and the similarity between the lives of the two John Henrys was hard to ignore.

The legend originated toward the end of the nineteenth century among railroad and tunnel workers. The details of the legend are just that—legendary—but the scholarly consensus is that something like the events of the legend happened, probably in the late 1870s near the Big Bend Tunnel in West Virginia. In the legend, John Henry is known far and wide for his amazing strength and endurance in driving railroad spikes. He is eventually enticed into a contest with a steam-powered spike-driving machine, and an epic contest ensues. They go neck and neck for several days. Then, in the final stretch, John Henry spurts to victory with a flurry of blows from his nine-pound hammer. His victory, however, exacts a terrible price. John Henry collapses from exhaustion and dies only seconds after crossing the finish line—a lesson for the industrial age.

For Sherman James, listening to the trials of a new John Henry and knowing the state of his health, the legend was more than a legend; it was a metaphor for a psychosomatic syndrome that might contribute to higher rates of black hypertension. James already knew S. Symes's conjecture, in the 1970s, that "prolonged, high effort coping with difficult psychosocial stressors could be the most parsimonious explanation" for greater hypertension among poorer populations, including blacks. Although John Henry Martin—James's new John Henry—had overcome many disadvantages, the intense and prolonged effort it took to do so may have taken a toll on his health. James saw the plight of John Henry Martin as emblematic "of the larger plight of African American men and women (especially those in the working classes) trying to free themselves from pervasive and deeply entrenched systems of social and economic oppression" (p. 169). He set out to test the "active coping/hypertension" hypothesis. In tribute to the "historical drama that he saw John Henry Martin's life to be a part of," he referred to it as the John Henryism hypothesis.

James first developed a scale to measure the values that make up John Henryism. It includes twelve statements such as "I've always felt that I could make of my life pretty much what I wanted to make of it" and "When things don't go the way I want them to, that just makes me work even harder." Respondents rate their agreement with each statement on a five-point scale. James hypothesized that coping with the stress of being low-income and black would be stressful for everyone, but that it would be especially stressful for those who scored high on his scale, that is, those in this group "who would persist with effortful active coping under difficult conditions." Measured this way, John Henryism sounds like the attitude of people who show stereotype threat effects—people who are identified with, and care a lot about succeeding in, an area where their group is negatively stereotyped.

James first tested this hypothesis with a small sample of black men from Pitt and Edgecombe counties, in North Carolina—two counties that, with some exceptions, were low-income and rural. Each participant filled out a John Henryism scale and had his blood pressure measured. That was all there was to the study. James's guess was right: men who scored high in John Henryism generally had higher blood pressure than men lower in John Henryism, and this effect was stronger among poorer than among better-off men. Further studies in the same counties used bigger samples and found the same thing. One study in Pitt County included 1,784 participants between twenty-five and fifty years of age. It found that among blacks in the lower third of the income distribution, those low in John Henryism had only a 19.3 percent incidence of hypertension, while those high in John Henryism had a 35 percent incidence.

The formidable conditions faced by low-income blacks in this rural area were not enough, by themselves, to elevate blood pressure. For that to happen, people had to be high in John Henryism beliefs; they had to care about succeeding enough to endure a struggle against difficult conditions. Race was a factor, too. Whites who lived under these conditions and were high in John Henryism did not show elevated blood pressure. It was high John Henryism pitched against the conditions of being poor and black in these rural, southern areas that raised blood pressure. Recent studies have found similar effects even among middle-class blacks.

6.

The research in this chapter has a daunting, if perhaps obvious, message: caring about doing well in areas where your group is disadvantaged, discriminated against, and negatively stereotyped can extract a price, sometimes a very heavy price. You may have no choice but to care. It would be difficult, for example, not to care about succeeding enough in society to become economically secure—the presumed motive of the high–John Henryism participants in Sherman James's research. There are costs even when the only barrier you face is being negatively stereotyped. That is what the experiments on stereotype threat's physiological effects show. Even the mild and short-lived doses of stereotype threat that can be implemented in these experiments are enough to raise your blood pressure, dramatically increase ruminative thinking, interfere with working memory, and deteriorate performance on challenging tasks. And if you continue for a long time to care and strive in an area where your group is negatively stereotyped, disadvantaged, and discriminated against, your acute reactions may turn into chronic health problems—with hypertension high on the list.

Ted experienced acute identity threat in his African American political science class. He didn't fully understand what was happening. But he could report intense symptoms—extreme nervousness, racing mind, lack of confidence about ordinary things, even about saying his name. The immediate effects of the threat were intense, but for Ted they were short-lived. Suppose they lasted for a long time. Suppose that, in order for him to achieve his basic life goals, he had to spend a major portion of his life in settings where, because of one of his identities, he had to endure the threat he experienced in this class. He'd get used to it, to some degree. He'd develop coping skills. He'd bond with others in the same identity boat. Still, he'd have to deal with this threat on an ongoing basis. It wouldn't be too much to expect that, after a while, he'd begin to pay with his health.

Even then, like John Henry Martin, he might be willing to pay these costs, so strong are the pressures to become economically secure and successful in society. But the truth is he would likely pay these costs with no better appreciation that he was paying them than the men who crossed the Capilano Bridge had of why they so liked the interviewer they met. Life's needs and goals are in the psychological foreground, the price of pursuing them in the background. We can't rely on Ted, or on the John Henry participants, to grasp the health costs they are paying as they pay them.*

To reduce those costs, we need to understand what makes them big and what makes them small, what makes the identity pressures that contribute to them worse, and what makes them better—the question to which I now turn.

---

*I want to be careful here. I don't want to imply that the pressure of identity threat and its cumulative impact on African Americans, even in intellectual areas, is so unmitigated and foreclosing as to allow only a few individual successes in these areas. There are clearly many such successes and many factors that can mitigate this threat for individuals. One can find oneself in intellectual achievement settings where stereotype threat is low (as we shall see, this can happen in settings where there is a "critical mass" of identity mates); one can find oneself personally treated as an exception to the stereotype; enjoying these benefits and having the requisite skills and motivation, one may achieve a level of public success that, itself, whistles Vivaldi and deflects stereotype judgment; one can have personal features (skin color, dialect and dress, etc.) that deflect stereotype judgment; and so on. And, I am sure that some John Henrys work hard enough to overcome the threat even under the worst of conditions. The point here, though, has been to reveal what it is that has to be surmounted for these successes to occur (this form of threat) and the fact that we may not always know the price we pay to do it.

CHAPTER 8

The Strength of Stereotype Threat: The Role of Cues

1.

On June 23, 2003, the U.S. Supreme Court announced its decisions in two landmark affirmative action cases in which the University of Michigan defended its right to consider the race of an applicant in admissions to its undergraduate school (*Gratz v. Bollinger*) and its law school (*Grutter v. Bollinger*). Weeks before the June 23 announcement, though, I was confident I knew what the decisions would be. I'd heard an interview of Justice Sandra Day O'Connor by Nina Totenberg on National Public Radio's *All Things Considered* on May 13. The common wisdom at the time was that the other eight Supreme Court justices would split evenly on these two decisions, leaving O'Connor's as the deciding vote on both.

Affirmative action was never mentioned in the interview. It focused on O'Connor's recently published memoir, *The Majesty of the Law*, which began with her youth on the Lazy B Ranch in Arizona and proceeded all the way through her time on the Supreme Court. When Totenberg asked O'Connor about her early years on the Court as its only woman, O'Connor said the experience was "asphyxiating." "Everywhere that Sandra went, the press was sure to go," she said, and noted that after each decision "there would be a little add on: What did Justice O'Connor do in the case?" Questions hung over her appointment: Was she good enough? Did she have feminist leanings? Was she insufficiently feminist? Hyper-scrutiny from all camps.

Then Totenberg asked O'Connor, "When Justice Ginsburg (the second woman appointed to the Court) arrived, it made things better?" O'Connor replied, "Oh, it was just night and day. The minute Justice Ginsburg arrived, the pressure was off. . . . We just became two of the nine Justices. . . . It was just such a welcome change." On hearing this as I drove along in my car, I felt I knew how the affirmative action decisions would go. I felt I knew because this statement revealed that O'Connor understood the concept of "critical mass," the basis of Michigan's defense.

The term "critical mass" refers to the point at which there are enough minorities in a setting, like a school or a workplace, that individual minorities no longer feel uncomfortable there because they are minorities—in our terms, they no longer feel an interfering level of identity threat. When Justice O'Connor was alone on the Court, she lacked critical mass. She was stressed, burdened with extra scrutiny, pressured to be the Jackie Robinson of women in the law. When Ginsburg arrived, she had critical mass. The stress and sense of burden subsided. The change was more than psychological. Her actual contingencies changed. The press sought fewer interviews with her after each Court decision; they asked her less about the "woman's perspective" in relation to decisions; they no longer followed her into restaurants. Her work environment now included someone who shared the experience and perspectives of being a woman. She could worry less about being seen stereotypically.

When O'Connor retired and left Ginsburg as the sole woman on the Court, Ginsburg lost critical mass, and her contingencies began to resemble those O'Connor had faced earlier. "I didn't realize how much I would miss her until she was gone," Ginsburg said recently of O'Connor's departure. "We divide on a lot of important questions, but we have had an experience growing up women and we have certain sensibilities that our male colleagues lack." Nor, she said, did she want the Court to signal that a woman justice is just a "one-at-a-time curiosity, not a normal thing." With O'Connor's retirement, Ginsburg's contingencies worsened. She had gone from being a "normal thing" to being not a "normal thing."

"Critical mass" is not a precise term. It's difficult to peg it to a precise number. O'Connor, for example, enjoyed a sense of critical mass with only one additional woman on the Court. Few colleges, however, would ever consider two minority students a critical mass. What's at play here? One possibility is that the number of minorities in a setting has to be large enough to improve the contingencies of individual minorities. Just two black students on a typical college campus would be just too few to affect the society of the school—the prevailing styles, who had status, who could be a student leader, the likelihood of being stereotyped, and so on. For example, would even 100 or 500 blacks be enough to achieve a critical mass on the University of Michigan campus of over 36,000 students? Yet adding one additional woman to a Supreme Court of nine justices changed O'Connor's contingencies dramatically.

The well-known Harvard organizational psychologist Richard Hackman and his colleague Jutta Allmendinger looked at this question in relation to the incorporation of women into symphony orchestras throughout the world. His findings were fascinating. In orchestras with a small percentage of women—in the 1 to 10 percent range—women musicians felt a lot like Sandra Day O'Connor on the pre-Ginsburg Supreme Court. They felt intense pressure to prove themselves and to fit a male model of what a good orchestra member is. Orchestras in which the percentage of women approached 20 percent or so—some degree of critical mass—still had problems, problems that were different from those when women were only tokens in the orchestra—greater gender fractiousness, for example—but problems nonetheless. It wasn't until the percentage of women in an orchestra reached about 40 percent that men and women alike began to report more satisfying experiences.

So it's hard to be precise about critical mass. Still, listening to the car radio that day in 2003, I knew that Sandra Day O'Connor understood that critical mass is real and important, despite its imprecision as a concept. She had lived its absence and its presence.

Justice O'Connor might have wished that the world was simpler: that we were all just individuals, that a given school or workplace was essentially the same situation for everyone regardless of her or his identity. She might have wished that being a lone woman on the Supreme Court was the same as being a man on the Supreme Court. She might have preferred an interpretation of the law that rigorously considered only the individual perspective, that recognized no contingencies of group identity. She was, after all, raised in the postfrontier West, a region known for its individualism. But she also knew her own experience. And in the end, on the Michigan decisions, she went with that. With O'Connor's as the deciding vote, Michigan lost the undergraduate school case (for using practices deemed too close to strict quotas) but won the law school case, which preserved universities' right to consider race as one of several relevant factors in the admissions decision—a signal from the Court that it considered a critical mass of minority students essential to these students' ability to function and learn in a university environment.

2.

Sandra Day O'Connor experienced intense identity threat in settings of great importance to her, such as the Supreme Court. The central question of this chapter is what makes this threat felt, and what determines how much a person is affected by it?

My first guess, as I've already confessed, followed my psychologist's inclinations. It must be something psychological, a trait perhaps, that makes one susceptible to the threat—a lack of confidence, an oversensitivity to the possibility of discrimination, a low capacity for dealing with frustration. But our early research had pointed in a different direction. The people most affected by this threat were people like Sandra Day O'Connor, Ruth Bader Ginsburg, and minority and women students at the achievement vanguard of their group. If still greater achievement skills were required to overcome this threat, then doing so could be next to impossible.

We therefore began to explore the role of circumstance. That's how we got to the idea of identity contingencies, those particular circumstances that went with a person's identity in specific situations. That led to the next idea: that what determines how much identity threat a person feels in a setting are the cues in the setting that might signal these contingencies—cues such as, in O'Connor's case, the greater attention her decisions received compared with the attention given to those of the other justices, the questions she got that seemed guided by gender stereotypes, and so forth. This became our working hypothesis about what makes identity threat felt, and what gives it the impact it has: more than individual traits, it is cues, contingency-signaling cues in a setting.

While we were thinking about this, I had an experience that vividly illustrated this idea to me. I visited a Silicon Valley start-up firm. Age cues were everywhere. The CEO was twenty-six years old, and the other employees were younger than he. Bicycles were hanging from hooks over employee's work cubicles. Music was playing that I had never heard before. I felt old. I imagined how I might feel if I worked there. I imagined worrying about my co-workers. They might have no general prejudice against older people, but in that situation they might see me stereotypically—as an "older person with no computer savvy." They might meet me with patronizingly low expectations or devalue my contributions. They might view me as being of little interest, or even worry that associating with me would cost them status, not sitting next to me in the cafeteria or at meetings. I could worry about all of these possible contingencies even if no person in the firm ever said a word. The bicycles hanging over the cubicles, or the kind of music in the air, the cues, would be enough.

This idea became our chief research question: Could it be that these cues—often innocent-appearing cues that seemed to be natural, unavoidable ingredients of a situation—regulate how much identity threat a person feels?

There are good reasons to think so. If you are "identity integrating" a setting—as O'Connor did on the Supreme Court, as Ted did in his African American political science class—then vigilance to possible contingencies is a central focus. And what more relevant information is there than features of the setting itself? You've often got nothing else to go on. It's no easy task. Any particular cue could tell you everything you need to know, or nothing at all. You have to keep delving, using multiple cues sometimes to triangulate on meanings. The number of phone messages Justice

O'Connor received from reporters after a Court decision could be telling her that her role in the decision is under special scrutiny—a contingency of her identity on the Court. Or an arguing attorney's tendency to make eye contact with only the male justices could be telling her that her sex detracts from her stature in the courtroom—another contingency. She wouldn't know for sure. These details could be telling her nothing. But at some level, explicitly or implicitly, she'd likely be sorting through them, trying to figure them out, and using valuable cognitive resources to do it.

We came to a simple working rule: if cues in a setting that point in an unsettling direction mount up, a sense of identity threat is likely to emerge. But if such cues are sparse in a setting and/or point in a benign direction, then a sense of identity threat should not arise or should subside. Rules are nice—if they work. In the chapters that follow, I hope this one will be useful in showing how to diminish identity threat, especially in places where its effects are deleterious. But for now, to convey the scope of the detective work that goes into figuring out contingencies, let me give a few examples of the cues I am talking about, a few of the major types.

Cues implicating one's marginality have to be high on this list. And the number one such cue is the number of other people in a setting with the same identity—the "critical mass cue." As Arthur Ashe, the African American tennis star of a generation ago once put it, "Like many other blacks, when I find myself in a new public situation, I will count. I always count. I count the number of black and brown faces present . . ." (p. 144). Ted counted the faces like his in his African American political science class, as did Ruth Bader Ginsburg on the Supreme Court. Virtually everyone has counted. Why? Because it tells us whether there are enough identity mates around that we won't be marginalized on the basis of that identity. It answers the "critical mass" question. A low count signals bad possibilities: that we might have trouble being accepted, that we might lack associates who share our sensibilities, that we might lack status and influence in the setting. It doesn't confirm these contingencies. It raises their possibility, which keeps us using our mental resources assessing likelihoods. Ted's being one of only two whites in his African American political science class, kept his vigilance on the boil all the time he was there.

Other cues, too, speak to marginality. If no powerful people in a setting have your identity, it tells you something. Perhaps your aspirations will be frustrated there. Perhaps you'll be pressured into marginal roles. An important thing about the presidential candidacies of Hillary Clinton and Barack Obama is that they helped politically demarginalize people of two major identities—women and blacks. No longer do these identities prevent access, in a categorical way, to the highest level of national leadership.

As a contingency detective, you may also notice how a setting is organized by identity. Is my cafeteria segregated by race? Are friendships at my school grouped by social class? Do the male professors get paid more than the female professors? Are most of the principals in my school district men? Is my access to resources—from the local swimming pool to knowledge of how to go about getting into college—affected by my family's wealth?

And then there are cues about a setting's inclusiveness. Does my school value the experiencing of group diversity as integral, or as marginal, to one's education? Is the school's leadership on the same page, or is there disagreement over this issue? Answers to such questions are contingency cues: they tell you what you may have to deal with in the setting.

And, of course, there are cues that signal prejudice in a setting. Is the expression of prejudice common, normative? Are some groups disdained in my workplace? Are people from different groups competitive with each other—on a group basis?

Several things about detecting identity contingencies are important to remember. First, you probably wouldn't do it unless you are "identity integrating" a setting. There may be some exceptions to this rule. Minority students in an all-minority school, for example, might read the school's dilapidation as a cue that the larger society devalues them. But, for the most part, it's the act of identity integration that occasions this detective work, that lights up the whole setting as a source of clues as to what identity contingencies you will have to deal with.

Second, this detective work isn't all about detecting prejudice. As I hope this list of "integration concerns" illustrates, not every identity threat comes from prejudiced people. Think about O'Connor on the Supreme Court before Ginsburg. Many of the contingencies she dealt with had little to do with prejudice among her fellow justices or her staff. Some of them may have been prejudiced, but her problems went beyond that: a Court that was dominated by male sensibilities and referents and that was less sensitive, in its functioning, to the perspectives of women; no critical mass of women with which to give her a sense of belonging on the Court; negative stereotypes about women in the larger society and in the legal world that were available for use in judging her work; the fact that her being the only woman on the Court made her the sole representative of her sex in each Court decision; and so on. O'Connor would have had to deal with these things even if there hadn't been an iota of sexism in any of the people she worked with.

It's sad, but true: identity threat is not the threat of prejudice alone; it's the threat of contingencies.

3.

As we did, you might have questions. Can a few cues in a setting really undermine a person's sense of belonging? Are people so attuned to the details of their social environments? We'd gotten to our ideas reasonably enough. When we stood back, though, our claim about the impact of situational cues looked strong. Would it hold up to an empirical test?

In developing these ideas, I worked primarily with two colleagues, Valerie Purdie-Vaughns and Mary Murphy. Although Valerie and Mary come from different backgrounds—Valerie, African American from New York City, and Mary, part Latina from Texas—their different backgrounds seemed to produce a shared talent: both had great psychological insight, and both were fascinated with how one's social identity affected one's everyday experience in workplaces and schools. We were joined sometimes by Paul Davies, an incisive, quick postdoctoral fellow from the University of Waterloo in Canada (currently a professor at the University of British Columbia, at Kelowna), and by Jennifer Randall Crosby, another smart, young social psychologist strongly interested in how identity shapes educational experience. Our team was excited by a question that might be called the "no man is an island" question: Can something as basic as our sense of belonging in a setting actually be affected by incidental cues in the setting—bicycles hanging from the ceiling, phone messages from reporters, being one of only two white students in a political science class—that only ambiguously signal identity contingencies? Our guts said yes, but we knew it was just as reasonable to assume that people can easily overcome the influence of such cues—if they want to, if, for example, the setting is important to them.

Our gut feeling was bolstered by new research findings. Michael Inzlicht and Avi Ben-Zeev did a study in which women took a difficult math test in groups of three test takers. In groups with no men, women did better than women in groups with one man; and in groups with one man, women did better than women in groups with two men. As the number of women in these groups went down—an incidental and ambiguous cue—so did their per-formance. These women were not "islands." They were affected by context; a background cue they might have been expected to overcome.

Our own Paul Davies, along with Steve Spencer, published another demonstration of the power of cues. They had men and women college students watch a set of six television commercials, ostensibly as part of a media study. For half of these students, two of the commercials included women depicted in silly gender-stereotypical ways—as a coed extolling the party life at her uni-versity, for example—and for the other half the commercials had no gender content. After viewing the commercials, each student was taken across the hall to an ostensibly different study where, to help a graduate, they could work on as many verbal and math items as they wanted to. The results were clear. The women who had seen the stereotypical images of women in the earlier com-mercials chose fewer math problems to work on, performed worse on the ones they did choose, and reported being less interested in math-related college majors and careers than women who had not seen these commercials. A completely incidental, passing cue—operating probably by evoking images of women that these women did not want to confirm—not only impaired their math performance but lowered their interest in math and math-related college majors and careers.

When I first saw these results, I wondered how well they would generalize to real life. Surely such passing cues could have only minor and passing effects. Then I remembered that in real-life situations like O'Connor's pre-Ginsburg Supreme Court, or Ted's African American political science class, or being a woman in a computer science class, the cues that cause these effects aren't passing, they're ongoing elements of the situation. As such, they might well cause major and lasting effects. We aren't islands: our life-shaping choices and critical performances can be affected by incidental features of our environments, even as we have little awareness of those features.

So now we had evidence that these cues, and the threat they caused, could impair performance and even make a person less interested in a career path. But we lacked direct evidence that incidental cues could make people feel they didn't belong in an actual setting, or that they couldn't trust the setting. Was this so?

Valerie Purdie-Vaughns and I came up with a simple experiment to find out. We gave samples of black and white respondents a lifelike newsletter ostensibly from a Silicon Valley company and asked them, after they'd read it thoroughly, to rate how much they felt they would belong in a company like that, and how much they would trust it. To see whether incidental features of the company, presumably by signaling possible identity contingencies in this workplace, would affect people's sense of belonging and trust there, we made up different newsletters—newsletters that included different company features—and then compared their effect on people's sense of belonging and trust.

Some of the newsletters included photographs of daily life that depicted a small number of minorities (blacks, Latinos, and Asians) in the company. In other newsletters these photographs depicted a larger number of minorities in the company. We wanted to learn the effect of another cue as well: the company's stated policy toward diversity. Some of the newsletters therefore included a prominent article stating that the company was strongly committed to "color-blindness"—defined as treating people, and trying to foster their welfare, as individuals. And some of the newsletters included a prominent article stating that the company was strongly committed to "valuing diversity"—defined as valuing the different perspectives and resources that people from different backgrounds bring to the workplace.

It was a simple procedure, and portable, too. We could hand out the newsletters to different samples of black and white respondents—to college students in the laboratory for sure, but also to business school students in a cafeteria, to an organization of black professionals at a TGIF mixer, and to perfectly innocent people riding the commuter train between Palo Alto and San Francisco. We used all of these different samples, and for all of them we examined the effect of the same two cues—critical mass of minorities and diversity policy—on how much they felt they would belong in the company and trust it.

The results were strong for virtually every sample we studied. White respondents (depicted as the majority group in our newsletters) felt they would belong in the company and trusted the company no matter what cues the newsletter contained—regardless of whether it depicted a small or moderate number of minorities in the company (the highest percentage of minorities we depicted was 33 percent) and of whether the company had a color-blind or valuing-diversity policy. Majority status, inside and outside the company, allowed a sense of belonging.

Black respondents, however, behaved a lot like Arthur Ashe: they counted. When the company was depicted as having a moderate number of minorities, they trusted it and felt they would belong in it as much as white respondents did. And they felt this way regardless of the company's diversity policy. Critical mass laid their vigilance to rest.

But when the company was depicted as having a low number of minorities, blacks' trust and sense of belonging were more conditional. Diversity policy became critical. Interestingly, the color-blind policy—perhaps America's dominant approach to these matters—didn't work. It engendered less trust and belonging. It was as if blacks couldn't take color-blindness at face value when the number of minorities in the company was small. But importantly, and just as interestingly, blacks did not mistrust the company when it espoused a valuing-diversity policy. With that policy in place, they trusted the company and believed they could belong in it, even when it had few minorities. The practical lesson here is that both critical mass and an approach that values what diversity can bring to a setting may go some distance in making minority identities feel more comfortable there.

The findings also reveal something more general: when people are appraising identity threat, one cue can shape the interpretation of another. A policy that explicitly valued diversity led black respondents to overlook the low number of minorities in the company, a cue that otherwise bothered them considerably. And depicting a larger number of minorities in the company led them to overlook concerns they would otherwise have had about a color-blind diversity policy. The meaning of one cue, then, depended on what other cues were also present.

Herein may lie a principle of remedy: if enough cues in a setting can lead members of a group to feel "identity safe," it might neutralize the impact of other cues in the setting that could otherwise threaten them. Once Ginsburg joined the Supreme Court, many of the cues in that setting that had made O'Connor feel such identity threat were still there—cues like the male-dominated culture and sensibility of the Court, the Court's history of all male justices, cultural suspicions about a woman's ability to be a good justice, and so on. But with Ginsburg there, O'Connor had enough identity safety—enough change in critical identity contingencies—that these other cues didn't bother her as much. She knew she was safer.

The studies Valerie and I did opened a possibility: to make a setting identity safe, perhaps you don't need to change everything, eradicate every possible identity-threatening cue, for example. Perhaps you could do it with a few critical changes, which by assuring a critical degree of identity safety could reduce the threatening meaning of the other cues. This is a point to which the next chapter returns.

But before exploring this idea, Mary Murphy wanted to take a deeper look at the impact of these cues. She had joined our lab with an interest in the mind-body relationship, the connection between psychological and physiological functioning. Her question was similar to the John Henry question: What was the *physiological* cost of identity threat? Did Sandra Day O'Connor and Ted pay a physical cost for enduring the cue-provoked threats they faced? Could incidental situational cues like the ones in the experiments that Valerie and I had done actually have physiological effects—that is, cause accelerated heart rate, elevated blood pressure, increased sweating as a sign of stress? We knew by then (see chapter 8) that experiencing stereotype threat while taking a test had such effects. But test taking is intense. Mary's question was about the physiological cost of identity threat in ordinary, everyday situations. If I had actually begun working at the Silicon Valley start-up firm, would the bicycles hanging from the ceiling have affected me *physiologically*? Did Ted have a physiological reaction to sitting in his African American political science class?

We needed help with this research. Mary went upstairs in our building and asked James Gross, one of the nation's leading researchers in the psychology and physiology of human emotions, to join the project. He's a very busy man, but he graciously agreed. Our little team was off, addressing the central question: Do incidental situational cues—cues that might signal threatening identity contingencies but that are completely incidental to the setting—actually affect people physiologically? To this question, we added another: Do these cues also make people more vigilant in the environment, more on the lookout for trouble? We could test their vigilance in the setting by testing their memory for its incidental features—the numbers of women and men there, where they were sitting, where the door was, and so on. The more vigilant they'd been, the more such features they should remember.

We brought men and women math and science majors at Stanford into the lab one at a time. Our stated purpose was to have them evaluate a video that advertised a math, science, and engineering (MSE) leadership conference scheduled to happen at Stanford the following summer. We were also interested in their physiological reactions to the video, we explained, and asked their permission to attach physiological sensors to their wrists while they watched it. The video presented photographs ostensibly taken at the preceding summer's conference. Some participants saw a "balanced" video, in which each photo contained one man for every woman. Others saw an "unbalanced" video in which each photo contained three men for every one woman, the cue that we thought might cause identity threat for the women viewers. After the video, via questionnaire, we measured all participants' memory for incidental features in the video and the experimental room— ending the experiment.

What happened? Not much for the men math and science majors. Their physiological reactions were unaffected by the gender ratio in the videos. They were calm throughout. Their memory for incidental features of the video and the setting were uniformly poor. Not so for the women math and science majors who watched the three-to-one video. Compared with the women who watched the one-to-one video and with the men, these women had dramatically elevated heart rates, blood pressure, and sweating, and they remembered more incidental features of both the video and the experimental room. They were aroused and paid more attention, presumably looking for contingency-signaling cues about the "leadership conference." A mere increase in the ratio of men to women was enough to strongly affect their physiological reactions, their vigilance in the setting and ultimately their memory.

Sandra Day O'Connor and Ruth Bader Ginsburg may not have realized it, but during their solo periods on the Supreme Court they likely carried an extra physiological burden, an unseen cost of the extra identity vigilance they were pressured into at the time. What Mary and I discovered is that it doesn't take much to cause this. It happens under very ordinary of circumstances. The difference between the three-to-one and one-to-one videos, if you weren't a woman in this experimental situation, would hardly be noticeable. Yet the three-to-one video was enough to quicken the pulse, elevate the blood pressure, and increase the stress of our women participants, as well as make them comb the video and experimental room for clues about things they might have to deal with as women in the world of math, science, and engineering.

Mary and I did other, similar experiments. They also showed the power of incidental, ordinary cues to cause identity threat. And they showed that the cues did this by making people worry about bad things they might have to deal with in situations on the basis of who they were. As important, these experiments reproduced the hopeful finding that Valerie and I had seen earlier: cues that signaled identity safety often quelled participants' identity threat, even when other cues in the setting still posed it.

We'd begun this research—Valerie, Mary, and I—looking for what determines the strength of identity threat. I think we found the answer. It is cues, features of a setting that signal bad identity contingencies. The more such cues there are, the worse the threats they portend, and the greater the chance the threats have of being realized, the more identity threat we feel. Sandra Day O'Connor's early days on the Supreme Court were saturated with these cues—not hate speech, not overt prejudice from her colleagues, just ordinary features of the Court and its context that signaled contingencies based on her gender—everything from the paucity of women's restrooms to stereotype-laden questions from reporters.*

So we had a working answer, one I liked because cues and contingencies are things that, at least some of the time, you can change. You can get your hands on them, and you can shape how people think about them. If identity threat were rooted in an internal psychological trait, a vulnerability of some sort, then it would be harder to remedy. Would there be enough therapists to go around? But environments, at least some of the time, can be changed. And the degree to which they are perceived as threatening can be changed as well. So I liked the answer we were getting. It offered insight into how identity threat, and its ill effects in important places, might be reduced. It gave us a clue as to how to think about remedy. It said focus on settings—their critical features and arrangements, their "inconveniences," as Bert Williams put it—and on how they are perceived.

With this understanding, I felt we had something that could improve the experience of identity integration in real-life settings. I hoped this was so, because that is the challenge we turned to next.

---

*To illustrate this reasoning in relation to minority schooling, one might expect stereotype threat to be more present for minority students at schools and colleges with more identity-threatening cues (small numbers of minority students, an intensely elite academic atmosphere, few minority faculty, etc.) than it is at schools and colleges with fewer identity-threatening cues (ample critical mass, a variety of ways of being successful, visible minority leadership, etc.).

CHAPTER 9

Reducing Identity and Stereotype Threat: A New Hope

1.

I n the fall of 1967 I began graduate school in the social psychology Ph.D. program at the Ohio State University in Columbus. The first thing to be said about graduate school—or medical school or law school, for that matter—is that virtually no one begins without some sense of intimidation, occasional displays of bravado notwithstanding. You're a "newbie" in a challenging, evaluative world in which you want to succeed. You read the available cues for evidence that you belong. Everybody does this. But being the only black student in my program, and one of only two or so in a psychology department of over one hundred graduate students, in an era when racial integration was still new to higher education, I had an extra layer of concern.

Did I match the image of the place? As graduate programs are supposed to do, this one stressed excellence: the values that defined it, the quality of work that embodied it. They were inspiring to me. But they came in a package—from my vantage point as a solo black, the package of an all-white program. Thus some of the incidental features of being white academics—the preference for dressing down, the love of seemingly all things European, a preference for dry wines, little knowledge of black life or popular culture—got implicitly associated with excellence. Excellence seemed to have an identity, which I didn't entirely have and worried that I couldn't get. Perhaps I could try for a while, but soon, I was sure, the veneer would wear off and the nonexcellent me would poke through. Many graduate students, I think, go through a version of this "imposter syndrome" as they try to assimilate into a professional culture. But when the difference in identities involved is racial, this kind of professional assimilation can seem nearly impossible.

A mean form of stereotype threat was also in the air. It was a place where intellectual ability was just about the most prized human characteristic, and it wasn't wasted on me that, in the American consciousness, this was precisely the characteristic my group was stereotyped as lacking. Lest I forget that, the science of psychology itself, like a child picking at a scab, keeps raising the question of whether blacks and whites have the same genetic intellectual capacity. In those days Arthur Jensen raised doubts in his paper entitled "How Much Can We Boost IQ and Scholastic Achievement?" Later it would be Richard Herrnstein and Charles Murray in *The Bell Curve*. Psychology poses this question with a seasonal regularity. And there I was, a specimen of the group in question.

It was hard to trust that behaving naturally, without careful self-presentation, wouldn't get me downgraded—seen in terms of bad stereotypes about my group, or as not fitting positive stereotypes of who excelled in the field. It was a broad pressure, not confined to difficult tests. I felt it in classes, in conversations, while sitting around watching football games. It could cause a paralysis of personality, especially around the faculty, even in informal situations like program picnics. I never asked a question in class. I felt like Ted in his African American political science class, except that the pressure wasn't confined to just one class. I remember once noticing my hands in the middle of a seminar. What did their darkness mean? Nothing? Everything?

It's important to stress that this didn't come from the hostility of those around me. Ohio State is a city of a university; my program was a friendly neighborhood within it. People generally pulled for one another. And for my part, I tried hard to interpret things in nonthreatening ways. But there was the constant task, in those early days, of figuring things out. Integration was hard work.

During this early phase of my time in graduate school, I lacked a narrative, an understanding of the situation that could inspire trust. It's not that narratives weren't available. There was the "try twice as hard and ignore what other people think" narrative, the civil rights narrative of patience and endurance, the "just have faith in yourself" narrative, and so on. I picked from all of these. But to reduce my tension, I needed a narrative that made me actually feel safer.

Something would happen to give me this narrative. And there's evidence that the same thing can help others in my predicament. But first comes a more basic question: Is identity threat that important? Is it a major cause of the group underperformance that launched this research journey, or is it just a minor contributor? Before dwelling on how to fix it, we should know how important it is to fix—in real colleges and universities.

2.

Bill Bowen is a man of famously prodigious energies. A midwesterner by birth, an economist by training, he was appointed from the faculty to the presidency of Princeton University in 1972, at the age of thirty-nine. He emerged as one of Princeton's most successful presidents and after leaving, in 1988, became president of the Andrew Mellon Foundation, which is known for its contributing heavily to American higher education as well as to the arts and humanities. As president of Mellon, Bowen was distinguished by a strong conviction: that major policy issues in higher education should be based, as much as possible, on empirical research. The research should address questions like the following: What background factors facilitate strong college performance? Are they the same for minority and low-income students? How much do the beneficiaries of affirmative action contribute to society later in life? How many academically strong students are displaced by the typical college's commitment to athletics? And he set out to show that useful empirical research on these issues could be done.

Bowen also had the persuasiveness and position power to get leading colleges and universities to provide the data needed for this research. He based his own research on the College and Beyond study, sponsored by the Mellon Foundation, which followed three cohorts of students at twenty-eight of the nation's selective colleges and universities—the classes of 1951, 1976, and 1987—from their college years into adulthood, often into their forties. On the basis of these data, Bowen and Derek Bok, a former president of Harvard University, reported in *The Shape of the River* that students admitted to those schools under affirmative action, even when they struggled "upriver" in college, often made stronger than average contributions "downriver," later in their lives—thus the title of their book.

During this time, the Mellon Foundation also funded another study of student experience in selective schools, this one conducted by the sociologists Stephen Cole and Elinor Barber. Both the Bowen and Bok and the Cole and Barber studies found strong evidence of minority student underperformance, the same phenomenon I had seen on that retention and recruitment committee at the University of Michigan lo those many years ago. Clearly the problem wasn't just Michigan's. But more important here, both sets of authors suggested that stereotype threat could be a cause. Bowen and Bok said this because underperformance in relation to white students was greatest among stronger black students, and since stereotype threat affects stronger students the most, maybe stereotype threat was involved. Cole and Barber said this because, looking only at strong students (their study investigated what led students into academic careers and thus focused only on stronger students), they found that underperformance was greatest at more elite schools, where they thought stereotype threat might be greatest. These findings could have other explanations, such as a lack of cultural capital or a lack of institutional know-how. I wondered. But for a long time, they provided the best evidence available on the real-life effect of stereotype threat on student performance—an effect that had been found so reliably in laboratory research.

Enter Douglas Massey and his colleagues, first at the University of Pennsylvania and then at Princeton University, who set out to directly measure the stereotype threat that black and Latino students experienced at selective colleges. Doug Massey has a lot in common with Bill Bowen: height, prodigious energy and productivity, and respect for careful research on society's hot-button issues—housing segregation and Latino immigration, to name just two. Again funded by Mellon, Massey and his colleagues launched a national study of college performance that was based, with few exceptions, on the same schools included in the Bowen and Bok study—most of the Ivies, large prestigious public universities, and distinguished liberal arts colleges. This time the focus was on how background characteristics of students influenced their performance in college. Playing on Bowen and Bok's title, *The Shape of the River*, they titled their first report *The Source of the River*.

Nearly four thousand students admitted to these schools— sampled in roughly equal numbers white, black, Asian, and Latino—were interviewed in person before they arrived on their respective campuses for their freshman year and again, by telephone, each spring through their junior year. This interview schedule meant the research team lacked measures of the stereotype threat students felt through most of their freshman year. They therefore measured background characteristics they thought might make a student susceptible to stereotype threat once on campus. Students were asked how much they doubted their own abilities, and how much they worried that professors and teaching staff would look down on their abilities. Students without these vulnerabilities could still experience stereotype threat, but the Massey team found that these vulnerabilities did affect early college performance among black and Latino students at those schools. So did the strength of academic preparation as measured by high school grades, the number of Advanced Placement courses taken, the family's socioeconomic status, the student's susceptibility to peer influence, and so on. Still, as the Massey team put it, "To a great extent . . . early differences in grades earned [between black and Latino students and the other groups] is explained by the different susceptibilities to stereotype threat and by the different levels of preparation for college that students in different groups bring with them when they arrive on campus" (p. 191).

So does the stereotype threat that black and Latino students actually experience on campus—as opposed to their susceptibility to it on entering college—affect their performance? The Massey team used the spring telephone calls to answer this question by asking, for example, how much they worried that their professors and others might see them stereotypically. They found that the more black and Latino students worried about these perceptions, the worse their grades got over the semester, and this was as true for students with low susceptibility to this threat as for students with high susceptibility to it.

Poor college performance has many causes, and the Massey team concluded that black and Latino students faced more such "causes" than their white and Asian counterparts. They were less likely to come from a two-parent home; their families were more likely to experience a distracting level of violence and trauma while the student was in college; these students were more likely to come from segregated backgrounds that gave them less access to the cultural knowledge and know-how that go into good college performance; the money they needed for college was a higher percentage of their family income; they were less likely to have gone to a high school with Advanced Placement courses; their precollege friendship networks were less likely to have been focused on college achievement; and so on.

Such findings show how disadvantages tied to race, class, and ethnicity—contingencies of identity, if you will—outside of college, extract a toll on performance in college. These students face "a thousand bites," as Massey put it. Still, like all of the Mellon studies, these studies found that stereotype threat had an undermining effect on college achievement that was in addition to the effect of those other disadvantages. This is a poignant fact. It means that even when black, Latino, and Native American students overcome other disadvantages in trying to gain parity with white and Asian classmates, they face the further pressure of stereotype and identity threats. Even privileged students from these groups have an extra, identity-related pressure working against their achievement.

The Massey team, however, did find something that alleviated this effect—black professors. Black and Latino students in these schools experienced virtually no stereotype threat in classrooms where the professor and probably more of the other students were black and Latino. The effect of "critical mass" again? As Ted said about the black students in his African American political science class, it just seemed that with so many more black students around, they felt freer of identity threat.

Stereotype threat, then, does affect the academic performance of minority students in real colleges. That's the point here. I expect that future research will find factors that moderate this effect—perhaps this pressure is greater in elite schools; perhaps it's less of a factor for first-generation immigrant minorities (who may not be seen as part of the stereotyped group); perhaps skin color makes a difference.

Nevertheless, the results that are in make it clear that identity threat is a significant cause of minority underachievement in American higher education, and is clearly worth "fixing," which brings me back to what changed my own experience of graduate school many years ago.

3.

I was assigned Thomas Ostrom as my faculty adviser, whose job it was to help me develop into a scientist through a research apprenticeship. Tom was soft-spoken and straightforward, with wispy hair that, when I met him, was in transition from the short hair of the early 1960s to the long hair of the late 1960s. From the vantage point of a new graduate student, he seemed mostly like a priest of scientific rigor. When we talked about research in his office, he often lit a fat white candle positioned prominently on his desk—and smiled hopefully.

Recall that, at the time, my personality was in full lockdown, especially at school. I did like meeting with Tom, though. He was calm, serious, and nice, but not that personal—which, to someone in personality lockdown, was rather welcome. He didn't seem worried about my paralysis. Maybe he didn't know what to do about it, or maybe he didn't even notice it. He didn't seem to focus on me. Rather, in the candlelight, it was the research that got his attention. It would be years before I got any direct praise from him, but his interest in what we were doing together was intense from the beginning.

I took a message from this: he had faith in me as a worthy partner. Somehow his assumptions about what he was doing as a scientist included me as, at least potentially, a capable colleague. My race and class identities didn't get in his way. If he'd given me praise, I might not have trusted it—so vigilant to threat was I. But I could trust this calm working relationship. My paralysis began to thaw. I teased him about playing the banjo. He pleaded with me that bluegrass music was really great and that I should give it a chance—knowing, beneath his wink, that for a kid from Chicago, this wasn't likely to happen. We laughed. My motivation intensified. I became as interested in the research as he. Tom liked that. We'd found an adhesive surface.

As this relationship came together, the same cues that had bothered me before—the constant references to who was "smart," the near-complete absence of minorities in the program or in the field, the faculty member down the hall who used the "N" word in class, the evidence that I was of a culture different from that which dominated the setting—bothered me less. I didn't like those things. But they didn't mean I couldn't fit into the field. At the level of the science itself, people could take my work at face value. My adviser did.

Tom had no knowledge of stereotype threat, or much knowledge of African American experience, for that matter. That wasn't the basis of our rapport, which rested, rather, on a straightforward, nice, but work-focused relationship that functioned like a cue of high critical mass (that is, high numbers of minorities or women in a setting) in the experiments that Valerie Purdie-Vaughns, Mary Murphy, and I did. It changed the meaning of the other cues in the situation.

Many years later, completely independently, a very thoughtful graduate student named Geoffrey Cohen—a person with a demeanor not unlike Tom Ostrom's—designed an ingenious experiment that actually put the Ostrom strategy of mentoring to an empirical test.

4.

Geoff is a social psychologist with an interest both in psychological theory—the understanding of basic psychological processes—and in putting psychology to practical use. As an undergraduate at Cornell, for example, he worked in educational programs for the disadvantaged and spent a semester of overseas studies on social problems and policy in Sussex, England. This side of Geoff led him to a practical and dramatic question: How does a white teacher give critical feedback to a black student so that the feedback is trusted and motivating?

One might first ask, Why would black students not trust the feedback in the first place? Let's view the situation from their perspective. The mere fact of being black, in light of the stereotypes about it, creates a quandary over how to interpret critical feedback on academic work. Is the feedback based on the quality of their work or on negative stereotypes about their group's abilities? This ambiguity is often a contingency of black students' identity. You might not really believe that an instance of critical feedback stems from stereotyping, or you might not want to believe it, but the possibility can't always be easily dismissed. And this makes the feedback difficult to accept completely. In this way, the quandary can isolate a student from valuable feedback. How do you give constructive critical feedback to students in this quandary? To find out, Geoff, along with Lee Ross—whom I introduced earlier—and I, designed one of the more labor-intensive experiments I've ever been associated with.

He brought black and white Stanford students into the laboratory one at a time and asked them to write an essay about their favorite teacher that, if good enough, would ostensibly be published in a new campus magazine on teaching. When they finished, they were told to come back in two days to get feedback on the quality of their essay. In that interim, Geoff and his colleagues actually read, grammatically corrected, and developed critical feedback for each essay—a task that, over the course of the experiment, often kept them up late.

When students came back two days later, they got critical feedback about their essay delivered in one of three ways; after that, they indicated how much they trusted the feedback and how motivated they were to improve their essay.

Two ways of giving this feedback didn't work as well with black students. It didn't work to try to be neutral. Nor did it consistently work to preface the feedback with a generally assuring positive statement. Unlike white students, black students didn't trust these forms of feedback, and, not trusting them, they weren't motivated to improve their essays. These forms of feedback, after all, could be covering some racial bias.

But one form of feedback did work, for both black and white students. I will call it the Tom Ostrom strategy. The feedback giver explained that he "used high standards" in evaluating the essays for publication in the teaching magazine. Still, he said, having read the student's essay, he believed the student could meet those standards. His criticism, this form of feedback implies, was offered to help the student meet the publication's high standards. Black students trusted this feedback as much as white students, and trusting it powerfully motivated them to improve their essay. For black students, the Ostrom style of feedback was like water on parched land—something they rarely seemed to get, but that, once they got it, renewed their trust and ability to be motivated by the criticism.

Why was it so effective? It resolved their interpretative quandary. It told them they weren't being seen in terms of the bad stereotype about their group's intellectual abilities, since the feedback giver used high intellectual standards and believed they could meet them. They could feel less jeopardy. The motivation they had always had was released.

This would seem to be what Tom Ostrom did for me. By demanding a lot, while at the same time believing I could meet those demands, he interrupted my worried narrative of the setting. And remember, the reason I had this narrative and needed this interruption is that the relevant stereotypes of my group, as well as countless features of the school, projected the idea that I wasn't the kind of person who belonged there. I don't believe I had this view because of some "psychic damage" that perhaps grew out of my experience of race in the United States, for example. The situation simply made the "I don't belong" narrative something that was hard for me to dismiss, as Ted's minority status did in his African

American political science class. What I had that Ted didn't have was Tom—someone in the setting whose manner of working with me could change this narrative.

Could this be a general strategy for improving the performance of ability-stereotyped groups? To answer that question, you'd have to take the strategy for a spin in the real world and see whether it is powerful enough to actually improve academic performance amid the pressures and complexity of actual college life.*

5.

Greg Walton was a graduate student of Geoff Cohen's at Yale in the early 2000s. He is now a psychology professor at Stanford. Like Geoff, Greg is a creative, committed scientist with broad interests, one of which is trying out social psychological ideas in

---

*As I write this, though, I can hear an important objection. Is it a good idea to talk someone out of worrying about something that could be a real threat to her or him? Wouldn't it leave the person less equipped to cope with the experience of being stereotyped when it happens? This is the dilemma faced by minority parents. Do they stress to their children the threat of discrimination, and risk making them too vigilant and worried to be comfortable in important places like school, or do they diminish this threat and risk leaving them too vulnerable to the fracturing experience of discrimination, should it happen? It's difficult to get this right. Reducing the threat a person sees in a setting may err in the direction of encouraging too much trust. But it may be worth the risk. I say this because it is hard to believe, in light of the central message of this book, that learning, achievement, and performance can be optimized without trust in the setting, trust of the sort that Tom Ostrom steered me to. An important finding of the research reported in this book is that the things people do in reaction to threat—vigilance to the setting, rumination, disengagement, and so on—are costly. They divert mental and motivational resources away from the learning and performance at hand. So while I know persons can be greatly hurt by the experience of prejudice—perhaps especially if they are not prepared for it—a greater threat may be the threat of impaired learning and underperformance that arises from the mistrust and disengagement it engenders. The worry about devaluation can be as costly as the devaluation itself. If one has to err, in light of our research over the years, I would thus err in the direction of urging greater trust, rather than greater vigilance.

the real world to see whether they can cause mountains to tumble into the sea.

The question they took on together was this: If you could somehow directly replace a highly vigilant-to-threat narrative, which might arise naturally from the cues of a college setting, with a narrative that offered a compelling hope about belonging and succeeding in the setting—would that be enough to improve students' college achievement? They devised a simple way to find out.

Imagine you are an African American student and you've been struggling along in your freshman year at a competitive university with a self-narrative of your experience that is much like the one I had during my early days at Ohio State. The place is saturated with cues that raise questions about your fit there—a small number of black and other minority students, few minority faculty and administrators, ethnic studies programs that are seen as of value primarily for minority students rather than for the general student body, an organization of social life that is heavily shaped by race, and so on. Accordingly, your narrative about the situation alerts you to the possibility that this school is not the right place for you to succeed and thrive.

Then one day, for a little less than an hour, you are shown the results of a putative survey of upperclassmen that summarizes, in narrative form, their social experiences at this university. The survey interests you because you want to see what students who are just like you, but a few years ahead of you, have experienced at this school. The results show that upperclassmen felt great frustration during their freshman year, just like you, even deep alienation from the school—in the sense of feeling they would never belong there—but that, over time, they gained a sense of belonging and happiness there, thanks to the resources and advantages of the school and the many lasting friendships they'd made there. The narrative conveyed through the survey makes your freshman frustrations look like passing troubles on the way to a hopeful future. Suppose also that you studied these survey results carefully enough to make the narrative a new narrative for your own experience. Would it weaken your vigilance-to-threat narrative, strengthen your narrative of belonging, and improve your academic performance?

When Greg and Geoff did exactly this experiment with freshmen at a northeastern university, they obtained a heartening result. Black students who got a brief narrative intervention of the sort I just described averaged one-third of a letter grade higher in the next semester than black students in a control group who got the results of a survey about political attitudes rather than about college life.

This is a promising result. Think of the long-term effects that a narrative intervention like this might have. If it improves black students' grades in an early college semester, then those better grades could further increase a student's sense of belonging, and that augmented sense of belonging could further improve grades— in a mutually reinforcing spiral of a trusting narrative fostering better grades, and better grades fostering a trusting narrative. As of this writing, preliminary follow-up evidence suggests that this may be just what happened.

Helping to shape the narratives that stereotyped students use to interpret their experience in a school may be a "high leverage" strategy of intervening. And there might be multiple ways of doing this. A study that my colleagues Steve Spencer, Richard Nisbett, Mary Hummel, Kent Harber, and I carried out in the early 1990s, at the University of Michigan, offers an example of a very different way of affecting narratives. In a dormitory-based academic program, we sponsored late-night bull sessions in which students in groups of no more that fifteen talked about topics of personal relevance—relations with parents and family, friendship and romantic concerns, experiences in their classes, fraternities and sororities, and the like. Reflecting the demographics of that university, black students were invariably a small minority of two, three, or four in these sessions. Yet they benefited most from being there, getting one-third of a letter grade higher than black students randomly assigned to control programs that didn't offer such sessions, and achieving close to the same grade point average as white students—those in the program and those in the control programs.

Why? Apparently the late-night talk sessions gave black students information they needed to have a more accurate and trusting narrative of their experience. The racial segregation of friendship networks in college life means that when it comes to personal conversations, blacks talk mainly to blacks and whites to whites. Black students, then, might not be able to see that white students have problems similar to their own. And not seeing this, along with being more racially vigilant in light of the broader cues in the setting, they might see race as playing a bigger role in their experience—as something that would sustain greater vigilance toward the racial aspects of their experience. The talk sessions corrected this. They revealed that the stresses of college life—a lower test grade than expected, an unreturned telephone call to a teaching assistant or classmate, an unfriendly interaction with another student, a chronic shortage of cash, and so on—happen to everyone regardless of race. This fact changes black students' narrative; it makes racial identity less central to interpreting experience and increases trust in the university environment. Having a narrative that requires less vigilance leaves more mental energy and motivation available for academic work and thus improved the grades of black students in this program.

The idea that modifying the academic narratives of ability-stereotyped students can improve their real-life grades is illustrated, in yet another way, by an ingenious study that Joshua Aronson, Carrie Fried, and Catherine Good did several years ago. They wanted to reduce the impact of stereotype threat by subtly teaching black and white Stanford students a more expansive narrative about intelligence. This idea came from the research of the Stanford psychologist Carol Dweck and her students on how our personal theories about ability affect our capacity to take on challenge—in school, at work, in sports. Dweck and her students focus on two theories in particular: the "incremental" theory, which frames the ability required to meet a challenge as learnable and incrementally expandable, and the "fixed" theory, which frames the ability as a fixed capacity that can't be meaningfully expanded but that can nonetheless limit one's functioning—the "either you have it or you don't" theory that many people hold about intelligence. Here's Carol's description of her own sixth-grade classroom:

> [M]y teacher seemed to equate worth with our IQ scores. We were seated around the room in IQ order. If you didn't have a high IQ, she wouldn't let you clean the blackboard erasers, carry the flag in the assembly, or carry a note to the principal. . . . The lower IQ students felt terrible, and the higher IQ students lived in fear that they would take another IQ test and lose their status. It was not an atmosphere that fostered . . . challenge.

When a stereotype indicts the intellectual abilities of your group, the implication is that, as a member of that group, you are like the lower-IQ students in Carol's sixth-grade classroom—you lack a critical fixed ability. It's a narrative that makes any frustration a plausible sign that you can't do the work, that you don't belong there. And it discourages your taking on academic challenges, for fear you'd confirm the fixed limitation alleged in the stereotype.

The question that Joshua, Carrie, and Catherine asked was whether the impact of stereotype threat could be reduced by giving students a narrative of intelligence as more expandable. Such a narrative would frame academic frustration as a fixable problem rather than as an unfixable limitation, thus reducing the risk involved in confirming the stereotype.

They devised a clever way to do this: they asked black and white Stanford students to write letters to ostensible minority elementary school students in East Palo Alto, California, advocating an expandable view of human intelligence. They were given information documenting the expandability of human intelligence; information on the nature of learning, on how the brain changes to reflect learning and experience, and evidence of people making great strides in building intellectual skills. And, of course, writing the letter gave them a chance to thoroughly process this narrative. For white Stanford students, not negatively stereotyped in this area, writing the letter had no effect on their subsequent grades. For black Stanford students, however, living under the suspicion of negative ability stereotypes, this changed narrative increased their grades by one-third of a letter grade in the next semester.

Sometimes you can give people facing identity threat information that enables a more accurate and hopeful personal narrative about their setting. When this is possible, these intriguing experiments show, it improves the academic achievement of people in real colleges; it can put their achievement on very different trajectories.

6.

Still, this research was done with strong students admitted to selective colleges. Would reducing identity threat also help the academic performance of ability-stigmatized students in K through 12 school-ing? Fortunately, we now have some answers to this question.

But there is, first, a more basic question: Are young children psychologically sophisticated enough to experience stereotype threat? Can they comprehend some prospect of being negatively stereotyped on the basis of being a girl or being black?

As it turns out, I have already presented evidence to this point. Remember the psychologist Nalini Ambady, who tested the effect of stereotype threat on young Asian girls' math performance in Boston. The girls in the youngest group in her study were five to seven years old. She gave all participants an age-appropriate math test. Gender-related images were evoked for some by having them color in a picture of a girl their age holding a doll just before taking the test. The five- to seven-year-old girls who colored this picture did significantly worse on the test than those who colored in, just before the test, a landscape drawing or a drawing of Asian children eating rice with chopsticks. So there it is. Girls as young as five to seven were thrown off their math performance by a cue as small as an ordinary drawing of a little girl holding a doll. They seemed well able to sense how their group was perceived in math.

Also, two Italian researchers, Barbara Muzzatti and Franca Agnoli, found that a similarly incidental cue (passingly presented classroom information that men have been dominant in high-level math) was enough to impair math performance in a sample of Italian girls as young as ten years of age. And finally, a study by Johannes Keller and his colleagues found that stereotype threat depressed the math performance of sixth-grade girls in Germany.

Evidence like this shows that young children do seem to have the psychological development needed to experience stereotype threat, at least by five or six years of age. As it does for adults, it impairs their performance in areas related to the stereotype. Its capacity to do this means that it can have lifelong cumulative effects—for example, deflecting women away from an interest in math before they've had much of a chance to engage it. And how much it does this—the strength of this pressure—seems to depend, as it does for adults, on the density of cues in the setting that evoke stereotypical images.*

But there is a still stronger way to test the role of identity threat in causing race, gender, and class gaps in test scores among K through 12 students: the same way this question was tested in higher education—by means of intervention research. You go into real schools and do something—an intervention—that you expect will reduce identity threat among stereotyped students. If nothing happens—and you've done a good job of implementing the intervention, and you've tried it perhaps several times—then identity threat is probably not an important cause of these gaps in that setting. But if what you do makes the gaps smaller, then you know that identity threat is a significant cause of these gaps in that setting, and you know one specific thing you can do to reduce those gaps. A number of people I have already introduced—Geoffrey

---

*The idea that the amount of identity threat a student feels in school depends on the density of cues in the school that evoke the threat has an interesting implication. It implies that this threat might actually be weaker in identity-segregated schools, where most of the students have the stereotyped identity in question—all-girls schools or classes, in the case of the math stereotype, or schools with virtually all low-income, minority students, in the case of race and class stereotypes. This is because in schools like these the identity is shared by everyone. That fact can make the students feel safer from being judged in terms of negative stereotypes about their group. It doesn't guarantee complete safety. Other cues in the setting—pictures on the wall, the degree of representation of that identity in curricular materials, the expectations and support of teachers, and the like—can still cause identity threat even in identity-segregated settings. Nor am I advocating single-identity schools or classes. Such a strategy could have downsides, such as how well students schooled in such settings fare in later, more integrated settings. And a central hope of our research is that identity-integrated settings can be made identity safe for all students. But on the principle that even when a strategy is not universally useful it may be useful in specific situations, I note that identity threat can be much reduced in identity-segregated settings.

Cohen, Joshua Aronson, Catherine Good, and Carol Dweck—and one person I am about to introduce, Julio Garcia, tried this strategy in what I regard as an extraordinary scientific turn, a revealing series of elegant, sometimes poignant intervention studies in K through 12 schooling.

7.

Geoff Cohen and Julio Garcia met as graduate students in the social psychology program at Stanford during my first years there. You've met Geoff, but not yet Julio. A Mexican American who grew up in Sacramento, California, in a middle-class family that owned an avocado ranch in Mexico, Julio has the comfort of a native in both the United States and Mexico—and a psychologist's fascination with human nature. Geoff and Julio left Stanford, began strong research careers, met again, and over a series of conversations came up with a K through 12 intervention idea that both excited and worried them.

The idea was based on self-affirmation theory, which, as I described, was developed by an earlier generation of graduate students and me in the 1980s. It posits a basic human motive to perceive oneself as good and competent—in a phrase, as "morally and adaptively adequate." When that perception is threatened—by events, by how others judge us, or even by our own actions that fail to meet our standards—we struggle to repair that good image. If actual redress fails or isn't possible, we rationalize, we reexplain our actions and other events so as to produce a self-image of competence and morality.

The most convincing evidence of this process is that, after a self-image threat—for example, showing a person that he has contradicted himself in an important matter—you can preempt his image-restoring rationalizations by giving him a chance to step back, take a breath, and affirm a larger, valued sense of self. We called this opportunity to step back a "self-affirmation." Against this larger image of self-integrity, the particular provoking threat seems smaller and less probative, and the person feels less need to rationalize it away.

Geoff and Julio reasoned that identity threat is like the self-image threats described in this theory, essentially a threat to a student's sense of being morally and adaptively adequate. Cues in the classroom—like being in a possibly devalued minority group, having a bad stereotype about your group be constantly relevant to the important activities in the classroom, facing a group-based social organization that signals your marginality—can be an ongoing threat to your perceived self-integrity. This is how identity threat is hypothesized to work in real classrooms. It constantly unsettles one's sense of competence and belonging.

Thus their idea: Would simply giving ability-stereotyped students a chance to develop a self-affirming narrative in the situation reduce the threat they feel in the classroom? And if it did, would that improve their performance? Geoff and Julio liked this idea. It made sense theoretically. And if it worked, it would have immense practical value too, offering a broadly useful and inexpensive way to help reduce minority achievement gaps.

But could it work? Could something so transient affect something as deeply rooted as minority achievement gaps? To think so was pinning a lot on theory. As I've stressed, minority student achievement gaps have multiple causes, ranging from socioeconomic disadvantage and family dislocation to unsupportive subcultures, and many extensive school reform efforts have failed to make even a dent in these gaps, or to sustain the initial improvements they did achieve. Could a brief self-affirmation, then, be expected to reduce these gaps? So worried Geoff and Julio.

But not so much that they didn't try it out. Now accompanied by Valerie Purdie-Vaughns, whom I introduced earlier, and Nancy Apfel and Allison Master, students working with Geoff, they tested this idea in several racially integrated seventh-grade classrooms near Hartford, Connecticut. Close to the beginning of the school year, they asked teachers to give each student in their classroom an envelope with his or her name on it. Instructions in the envelope asked half of the students, randomly selected, to write down their two or three most important values (for example, family relationships, friendships, being good at music, or their religion) and then write a brief paragraph about why these values were important to them—that is, to put these value statements in the form of a personal narrative. This took only about fifteen minutes. When they were done, they put the material back in the envelope and handed it to the teacher. In later school terms, they did a few similar follow-up writing exercises That was it.

The other students in these classrooms—the control group— did the same thing, except their instructions asked them to write down their least important values and to explain why others might find them important. These students got a chance to think about values, but no chance to affirm any self-narrative about them. Could the brief self-affirmation affect school performance?

It did—dramatically so. The affirmation exercise improved the grades of all but the strongest black students over their performance in the first three weeks of school, before they did the affirmation. And those with the poorest early performance improved the most. They did better in the class where they made the affirmation and in their other classes too. Other measures showed that the affirmation even reduced how much they thought about the racial stereotypes over the entire semester. The results for the black students in the control condition—those who did no value affirmation—helped reveal what the affirmation did to reduce the gap. It stopped a slide in grades that otherwise would have happened. The grades of the no-affirmation control students kept going down, making the racial achievement gap in these classrooms ever wider over the school term. What the affirmation did for the black students who performed it was to stop or slow this decline. In so doing, it reduced the gap with white students by 40 percent over the term. Just as amazing, follow-up research showed their higher achievement, and thus smaller gap with white students, lasted for at least two years.

(The self-affirmation didn't help white students in this study. The authors explained it this way: "We would . . . expect this intervention to improve the performance of all groups of individuals subjected to a threat sufficiently pervasive and intense to impede that entire group's average performance." But, their argument goes, whites as a group didn't feel a threat based on their racial identity in this classroom. They might have felt such a "pervasive and intense" identity threat in an elite basketball camp with lots of black players around, but not in these classrooms, where they were a majority. So the apparent power of an affirmation to lift this threat had little effect on their average performance.)

Lots of people are amazed by these findings, perhaps to the point of doubting them. Okay, they might say, fifteen minutes of written reflection on one's self-defining values is probably a good thing. But how could it be enough to improve the grades of minority students in these classrooms, especially when so many more extensive efforts have failed? And how could its effects last for more than two years?

Such findings are a skeptic's delight. And when you are the scientist who has produced them, all you can really do is try to replicate them—which Geoff, Julio, Valerie, and their students have now done near Boulder, Colorado, with Latino Americans. A replication, however, raises even more the question of how this intervention works.

In answer, the researchers offer a two-part explanation. The first part is the self-affirmation idea. With one's larger sense of competence and worth brought into view by the writing exercise, poorer early performance in the semester and other identity-threatening cues in the classroom were less all-important than they would otherwise have been. This made students less vigilant, freeing up mental resources and improving performance.

The second part of their explanation is that better performance interrupts an otherwise negative recursive process, a process that stood out vividly among blacks in the control condition. Without an affirmation, early frustrations and threatening environmental cues worried them more, which worsened their performance, which worried them still more, until a full-scale downward progression was underway. In their words,

> African Americans, a stereotyped group, displayed greater psychological vulnerability to early failure [and, I would add, to other identity-threatening cues as well]. For them, early failure may have confirmed that the stereotype was in play as a stable global indicator of their ability to thrive in school. By shoring up self-integrity at this time, the affirmation helped maintain their sense of adequacy and interrupted the cycle in which early poor performance influenced later performance and psychological state. (p. 403)

If this book reveals anything, it's that understandings evolve with continued research. This will surely be so for the processes underlying the affirmation project. What social psychologists call "moderators" of the affirmation effect will doubtless emerge—

factors without which the salutary effect of affirmation on minority student grades won't happen. For example, perhaps affirmation will help grades in good schools with good instruction but not in poor schools with poor instruction. The authors stressed that the success of their intervention depended on good teaching and resources being in place in these schools. Reducing identity threat, they suggest, simply increased black students' access to that instruction. If quality instruction hadn't been available in these schools, affirmation might have had little effect. Or perhaps affirmation will help grades in integrated schools where identity threat is more of a factor, but not help grades as much in more identity-homogeneous schools where identity threat is less of a factor. I wonder, for example, about all-girl schools, or minority and low-income schools, where virtually everyone shares the ability-stereotyped identity in question. Stereotyped students may feel less likely to be judged and treated stereotypically in schools like these. (See the earlier footnote for a broader discussion.)

This said, the present findings make an important point: a psychological intervention that leaves minority students less susceptible to negative stereotypes about their group's abilities can significantly improve their performance in real schools for a long time. Identity threat isn't a passing threat that happens just on tests. It's a cloaking threat that can feed on all kinds of daily frustrations and contextual cues and get more disruptive over time. The fate of black control group students shows how profound these "social psychological" pressures are in real life. For integrated schools like the ones in these studies, the cloaking effects of identity threat can be a big part of the racial achievement gap—and reducing this threat is a necessary part of the solution.

If you take the intervention of Geoff, Julio, Valerie, and their colleagues as proof that something that does nothing more than reduce identity threat can improve performance by ability-stereotyped students, even for a long while, then you might want to know that it can be done in other practical ways.

And fortunately, it can.

Catherine Good and Joshua Aronson tested whether Carol Dweck's type of coaching—encouraging the view that abilities are expandable—could, by reducing the impact of stereotype threat in school, increase the grades and test scores of ability-stereotyped students. They randomly selected a sample of low-income and minority students from the entering class of a rural Texas junior high school, and assigned each of these students a college student mentor who advised them academically over the year, meeting with them twice and emailing them regularly. For one group of mentees, the mentors stressed the expandability of intelligence—regularly explaining how the brain makes new neural connections when it learns new things, and exposing them to a restricted website that showed illustrations of brain dendrites growing when a person tries to solve hard problems. Another group of mentees engaged in similar activities, but theirs were focused on drug abuse prevention rather than on the expandability of intelligence.

Which group performed better?

The Texas Assessment of Academic Skills (TAAS) was given at the end of the school year. Both girls and boys whose mentors had focused them on the expandability of intelligence did significantly better on the reading section of this test than those who had focused on drug abuse prevention. But the biggest effect of the "intelligence is expandable" message was for girls on the math section of the TAAS—the part of the test on which they would likely have experienced the greatest stereotype threat. Among students whose mentoring had focused on drug abuse prevention, girls scored significantly lower on this section of the TAAS than did boys—reproducing the typical gender gap in math performance. But among students who focused on the expandability of intelligence, girls performed at the same level as the boys on this section—completely eliminating the usual sex difference on the test.

8.

These studies show that affirmations, incremental mindsets, and the like can steer ability-stereotyped students in K through 12 into self-narratives that—like mine at Ohio State—deflate the threatening meaning of environmental cues. One might then ask—as my wife, Dr. Dorothy Steele, did—whether you could find further techniques for doing this if you studied the behavior of teachers who, compared to their colleagues, were especially good with ability-stereotyped students. Would their practices reveal a strategy for creating "identity safety" and improving grades? Eventually she talked a number of us—including Hazel Markus, a leading social psychologist and pioneering founder of modern cultural psychology; Paul Davies, whom I introduced earlier; Amanda Lewis, an esteemed educational sociologist at Emory University who was visiting Stanford as this project began; Francis Green, a topflight research manager; and me—into helping her conduct a study of this question in the elementary school classrooms of Richmond, California, where most students have one or another ability-stereotyped identity, where specifically the breakdown of student ethnicities was 33 percent Latino, 32 percent African Americans, 17 percent white, and 12 percent Asian (and 6 percent other ethnicities), and where the vast majority of students came from low-income families.

The study plan was simple: we would observe teachers in their classrooms and measure as many of their practices and as many features of their classroom culture as we could, and then see which practices and features enabled their students to feel more identity safety and to perform better on year-end standardized tests.

Trained observers, not informed about identity safety, observed third- and fifth-grade teachers in eighty-four classrooms in thirteen Richmond elementary schools. Each teacher was observed three times during the year and rated on a variety of scales, such as "positivity of relationship with students," "child-centered classroom decision-making," "use of high expectations and academic rigor," "degree of stress on fundamental skills," "teacher skill," and "teacher restrictiveness," nineteen scales in all.

A distinct constellation of teacher practices and classroom features emerged that fostered identity safety and better performances on year-end tests. The effect of this constellation was somewhat stronger in the fifth grade than in the third. But it included the same things in both grades: positive relationships with students; more child-centered teaching; use of their diversity as a classroom resource rather than following a strict strategy of colorblindness; teacher skill, warmth, and availability; and so on. Interestingly, top-down decision making with a stress on basic skills didn't work well in these schools. In Dorothy's words, the effective, identity-safe practices "avoid cues that might instantiate a sense of stereotype threat in students and are, instead, aimed at making everyone in the class feel . . . as valued and contributive . . . regardless of their ethnic group or gender."

9.

At this point, then, accumulating research shows that reducing identity threat or its impact in integrated K through 12 schools improves the academic performance of ability-stereotyped students, as it did for ability-stereotyped students at the college level.

The benefits are sizable, reliable, and often long-lasting. And the interventions themselves are low cost and relatively easy to do. Their cohering principle is straightforward: they foster a threat-mitigating narrative about one's susceptibility to being stereotyped in the schooling context. And though no single, one-size-fits-all strategy has evolved, the research offers an expanding set of strategies for doing this: establishing trust through demanding but supportive relationships, fostering hopeful narratives about belonging in the setting, arranging informal cross-group conversations to reveal that one's identity is not the sole cause of one's negative experiences in the setting, representing critical abilities as learnable, and using child-centered teaching techniques. More will be known in the years ahead. But what we know now can make a life-affecting difference for many people in many important places.

Still, one might ask how central should reducing identity threat be in efforts to help students with substantial skill and knowledge deficits relative to those of other students at their school? Schools sometimes admit students who have strong intellectual potential but who lack the educational background of other students at the school. Can efforts to reduce identity threat suffice to help these students?

No, would be my answer. Reducing identity threat is not sufficient to overcome real skill and knowledge deficits in school. To do that, students have to have the opportunity to acquire the relevant skills and knowledge. They need good instruction and the chance to apply themselves to critical material, sometimes for long periods of time. But it's equally true that for ability-stereotyped students, reducing identity threat is just as important as skill and knowledge instruction. It may not be sufficient, but it is necessary. That is, no amount of instruction, no matter how good it is, can reduce these deficits if it doesn't also keep identity threat low. Without that, threat will always have first claim on students' attention and mental resources. So neither approach—providing instructional opportunities or reducing identity threat—is sufficient, by itself, to improve academic performance, especially for ability-stereotyped students. Both are necessary.

That said, the intervention studies bear a profound lesson: even though group underachievement problems may be rooted in background factors that are difficult to change—socioeconomic disadvantage, poorer access to good schooling, less parental support, low participation in social networks that enable the timely development of critical skills and cultural capital, historically rooted patterns of sex-role socialization, and so on—remedying the immediate causes of these problems in the situations in which they occur can improve things dramatically. Heart attacks also have background causes that are difficult to change—genetic history, long-term habits of diet and exercise, smoking, life stress, etc. Nevertheless, the likelihood of a heart attack can be greatly reduced by drugs and surgery. They do nothing to counter the background causes of heart disease; they treat the most immediate cause of a heart attack, blocked coronary arties. There were many difficult-to-change, background factors that caused me distress in my early days at Ohio State—my different racial and social class background, the absence of a critical mass of other minority students, and so forth. You couldn't change these things, or change them easily, and so you could think there was nothing to be done for me. It wouldn't seem that a trusting relationship with a mentor, a white mentor at that, would make a difference. It wouldn't fix the things causing my troubles. But the point here is that it might reduce the troubles themselves.*

---

*These findings justify the hope that schools can do more than might be suspected to reduce achievement gaps. As I noted, this isn't a universally shared view. As James Heckman and his colleagues recently put it, "The Coleman Report as well as recent work . . . show that families and not schools are the major sources of inequality in student

And beyond this hope, the research of this chapter offers two strategies for reducing identity threat. First, realizing that this threat arises from cues in a setting that signal possibly threatening contingencies of identity, one can try as best as possible to eliminate those real contingencies and the cues that signal them. You can become alert to how the features of a setting affect people and change them so that they don't disadvantage certain groups. For

---

performance. By the third grade, gaps in test scores across socio-economic groups are stable by age, suggesting that later schooling and variations in schooling quality have little effect in reducing or widening the gaps that appear before students enter school" (p. 1901). And, of course, they could be right.

But maybe not entirely. The analyses underlying Heckman's view are reasonable. They take factors that are typically associated with school quality like funding per pupil, classroom size, and education level of the teachers and test whether differences between social classes and races on these factors—the fact that middle-class children may go to schools with smaller class sizes, for example—actually cause the differences between social classes and races in school performance and test scores. And when they find that they don't—when they find, for instance, that the racial gap in test scores still exists even for black students in schools with smaller classes, better teachers, and more funding—they are pushed to conclude that the race gap in school quality is not the cause of the race gap in test scores. Something else must be at work. And since these gaps are there as these kids begin school, before schooling has had a chance to affect their skills, they must be caused by group differences in child rearing. That's how they get to the idea that the quality of schooling isn't as important as families in causing these gaps.

Reasonable. But here's the problem: suppose a part of schooling that actually contributes to these gaps is something the researchers didn't know about and didn't measure. If they didn't measure such a factor, but did measure factors that don't contribute to the gaps, their analysis could reach the wrong conclusion that school quality doesn't matter, when what their research really shows is that the things they've measured as school quality don't matter. Another dimension of school quality could well matter, perhaps in a major way.

And the intervention studies suggest that another dimension of school quality might be a schooling climate, a mode of instruction, or a relationship that fosters a narrative of trust in the setting. These studies show that when this threat is subdued for ability-stereotyped students, their performance goes up, and that, in turn, can launch a positive recursive process of good performance protecting against further identity threat, which allows further good performance, until the gap between these and other students is reduced. That's why it's a dimension of schooling quality. It's necessary for ability-stereotyped students to benefit from quality teaching and resources.

groups. For the sake of the few over-forty types working in that Silicon Valley start-up firm that I visited, maybe all of the music wouldn't have to be the "Indie rock" and hip-hop preferred by the under-twenty-five-year-olds. For the sake of minority students in college, perhaps the curriculum considered "core"—and thus of foundational value for all students—could include in-depth material reflecting the history and perspective of multiple groups in American society.

Second, the intervention studies show that, when the effort to change identity-relevant cues and contingencies in a setting can go no further, helping people understand the safety they do have in a setting is immensely valuable—academically valuable. And they demonstrate intriguing ways of doing it, ways that I hope will be suggestive.

10.

The intervention studies were done to test whether reducing stereotype threat, or the subjective sense of it, would improve real-life grades. As they began to accumulate, however, Greg Walton and Steven Spencer saw that these studies could also be used to examine two other questions: whether stereotype threat is a significant cause of stereotyped students' underperformance in real schools* and whether our traditional measures of academic potential (for example, the SAT) might, at least under some circumstances, underestimate the potential of stereotyped students. Addressing these questions brings the research of this book full

---

*Recall that underperformance is that part of a group performance gap that is due not to differences in skills and knowledge between the groups but to something that has eluded explanation.

circle—it was the puzzle of minority student underperformance that started this research. Greg and Steve saw that answering these questions boiled down to deciding between two scenarios of how identity threat affects an earlier test performance and the later grade performance it is used to predict.

The events of both scenarios are the same. Imagine you are a black high school student applying to college. You take the SAT, you score less well than you'd hoped to, but because your score is okay and you have other strengths, you get into a competitive college. In college, however, your grade performance is again lower than you expected—lower, in fact, than was predicted by your SAT, that is, lower than other students with the same SAT score. In other words, you underperform in college. The events are the same, but the interpretation of what caused them is where the two scenarios differ.

In scenario one, stereotype threat doesn't much affect your earlier test performance or your later college grades. The prior test (or prior grades) is a valid assessment of potential for people of all identities. Individual and group differences in performance on it are assumed to reflect individual and group differences in underlying academic skills and knowledge. And the reason a group might underperform in college is assumed to be something like the lesser motivation of its members.

In scenario two, both the earlier test performance and your college grades are depressed by stereotype threat. Thus the earlier test performance underestimates your true potential, not necessarily because of biased content, but because of the interfering pressure of stereotype threat during the test. And what happens when you get to college, in this scenario, is that escalating identity threat in the college environment drives your performance even lower than that underestimation would have predicted.

Which scenario is correct?

The first scenario has the fact of black student underperformance on its side. If a prior test like the SAT underestimates your true potential because of stereotype threat, then your true higher potential might be expected to shine through in later coursework, meaning that your later grades should be higher than those of nonstereotyped students who got the same SAT scores you got. But this doesn't happen. Black student underperformance, as you know, shows that black students don't typically get higher subsequent grades than nonstereotyped students with the same SATs; they typically get lower subsequent grades than these nonstereotyped students. So, in scenario one, the prior test, the SAT in this example, didn't underestimate your potential. If anything, it overestimated your potential, since you never got grades as high as it predicted.

Greg and Steve's realization was that you could actually test empirically which scenario was correct—at least for the sample of students who had participated in the intervention studies designed to reduce stereotype threat. All you would need for these students was their earlier test scores and the college grades they earned while in the program.

If stereotyped students got better subsequent grades than nonstereotyped students when they were in an intervention program, then scenario two would be supported. For example, if alleviating stereotype threat in college led stereotyped students to "overperform" there in comparison to nonstereotyped students, it would mean that their underperformance in more typical college environments was likely due to the stereotype threat in those environments depressing their grades. It would also suggest that the earlier test of their potential, say, the SAT, underestimated their true potential since they actually got higher grades than the test would have predicted when stereotype threat was reduced in their later college environment—higher grades than nonstereotyped students with the same SAT scores, for example.

But if stereotyped students continued to get worse grades than nonstereotyped students in a program that reduced stereotype threat at their school, it would mean that stereotype threat had no effect on either their school grades or their earlier test performance. It would mean that scenario one was correct.

A clear test was on.

Greg and Steve gathered the intervention studies for which they could get participants' prior test scores or prior grades (as a nontest measure used to predict later school performance) and subsequent grade performance during the intervention—Greg and Geoff's study at the university in the Northeast; Geoff, Julio, Valerie, and their students' studies in the grade schools of New Haven and Boulder; and the study my colleagues and I did at the University of Michigan.

The results were clear; scenario two carried the day. In these interventions, stereotyped students consistently got *better* subseqent grades than nonstereotyped students with the same prior test scores or grades. They not only didn't underperform; they "overperformed."

In science, one must be cautious. Maybe these interventions did something in addition to reducing stereotype threat that led stereotyped students to perform so well. I can't think of what that could be—certainly not something that could explain the full pattern of their results. Further research will, of course, be more penetrating.

But having gestured to caution, several things are especially impressive about these findings. Considering how modest these interventions were, their impact was dramatic. They show that, at least in these samples, even modest attempts to reduce this threat totally eliminated the classic pattern of minority student underperformance—a strong indication that this underperformance was being caused by stereotype threat. They also suggest that the earlier-taken measures of potential used to predict later performance (such as the SAT in the college-level interventions and prior grades used in Geoff, Julio and Valerie's middle school intervention) were themselves biased; that is stereotype threat suppressed the performance of stereotyped students on these measures causing these measures to underestimate the potential of stereotyped students—a potential that got revealed in a later school environment that reduced this threat.* Nor are

*Researchers at the Educational Testing Service (ETS), who make tests such as the SAT and the Graduate Record Exam, have tried to evaluate the effect of stereotype threat on real-life standardized test performance. In perhaps their most extensive effort, they had test takers record their race and gender either before or after taking the Advanced Placement (AP) exam in calculus. One might expect that stereotype threat during the test would be greatest for stereotyped students who listed their stereotyped identity before, rather than after, the exam—thus allowing the identity, and stereotypes about it, to shadow their performance. And in fact, women in this study who recorded their gender before the AP exam scored significantly worse than women who recorded their gender after the exam, but the ETS team said this effect was less than "psychologically significant." A later reanalysis of the data by two University of Kansas social psychologists, Kelly Danaher and Chris Crandall, countered this conclusion with the calculation—based on the size of the effect in this study—that if gender were routinely recorded after this AP exam, rather than before it, as many as 2,837 more women (out of 17,000) would start college every year with calculus credit, and they would have had better admissions chances. For black students the trends were in the same direction but didn't reach conventional statistical significance.

These results are difficult to interpret, however, because of a serious methodological problem: on real-life, high-stakes standardized tests like an AP exam, you can't find a control group of stereotyped students who would plausibly not experience stereotype threat on the test, and who could thus provide a base rate of performance under no stereotype threat against which you could compare the performance of stereotyped students who experience the threat. (The difficult part of developing stereotype threat laboratory studies was not in creating stereotype threat for ability-stereotyped students but in coming up with techniques to get rid of stereotype threat on stereotype-relevant tests for ability-stereotyped students—something that is nearly impossible to do in real-life testing situations, because you can't control how real test takers interpret the test.) Given the high stakes of the AP exam, all stereotyped test takers likely experienced a good deal of stereotype threat on this test regardless of whether they recorded their stereotyped identity before or after the test. This experiment, then, compared groups that, in all likelihood, both experienced stereotype threat, probably lots of it, and such a comparison just can't tell you how much of a damaging effect stereotype threat per se had on performance.

these passing findings. The studies in Greg and Steve's analysis included students of different ages—both K through 12, and college-age students—several different strategies for reducing stereotype threat, and many hundreds of student participants in all. These findings show the cumulative effect of stereotype threat, as an identity contingency, on the intellectual development, over time, of an entire group of ability-stereotyped people. And it shows what to do about it, that environments can be feasibly modified to allow ability-stereotyped students the kind of unencumbered engagement with academic work needed to fulfill their potential.

This research journey has been long, and it's far from over. But it has reached a marker. A preponderance of evidence strongly suggests that underperformance, when not caused by discrimination against a group in grades, is likely caused by stereotype and identity threats and the interfering reactions they cause. It also suggests that tests used to measure students' potential for some subsequent level of schooling, under a common set of testing conditions, can underestimate the actual potential of stereotyped students. This effect has been difficult to discern because the subsequent grade performance of these students is also depressed by stereotype threat, this time in the schooling environment itself. That these threats cause something as lawfully observed in American society as minority student underperformance means that they are as common as crabgrass, and just about as unruly.

Still, a hope arises from this research. If we want to overcome underperformance, if we want to open the door for many stereotyped students to learn and prosper in society, we should, in addi-

---

That is why the strategy that Greg and Steve developed is so important. It provides the most interpretable evidence of stereotype threat's effect on real-life testing to date, and it reveals that these tests consistently underestimate the true skills of ability-stereotyped students in these samples—a fact that has been hidden, as explained above, because stereotype threat suppresses both their test and later grade performance.

tion to focusing on skill and knowledge, also focus on reducing these threats in schools, classrooms, workplaces, even basketball gyms. You should focus on making the identity less "inconvenient." And this first era of intervention studies makes a good beginning in showing you how to do it.

But doing this requires that we Americans come together, across identity lines. We have to engage integrated settings to improve them. Yet to do that, we all may have to overcome still another form of identity threat —a form that, if ignored, would leave any understanding of the role these processes play in the larger society incomplete, a form to which our research next turned.

CHAPTER 10

The Distance Between Us:
The Role of Identity Threat

1.

In her illuminating book *The Failures of Integration*, Sheryll Cashin shares a private joke that she and her husband (both African Americans) have about flights on Southwest Airlines, which allows passengers to board on a first-come, first-served basis. If they arrive late, they hope for what they call "Southwest Airlines First Class." They hope that a young, dark-skinned African American male will be toward the front of the line and will take one of the comfortable, exit-advantaging seats toward the front of the plane when he boards. Cashin says, "At least four out of five times, we can depend on the seats next to that black person being empty, even if his row is far up front, begging for the taking. I am always happy to take this convenient seat, feeling grateful for the discomfort of others and marveling at the advantage they are willing to pass up due to their own social limitations. I smile warmly at my black brother as I plop down next to him" (p. 13).

What causes the Southwest Airlines First Class? Is it due entirely to the prejudice of white passengers, a racial aversion, perhaps, to being close to a black passenger? Or is it caused, in some part, by the predicament of identity that is at the center of this book, the same predicament that I suggested bottled up Ted in his African American political science class? These possible causes of the Southwest Airlines First Class are different, with different implications for what you'd do to reduce the tension and distance between groups.

The identity threat explanation doesn't require attributing prejudice to the white passengers. All one need assume, it says, is that they have a worry like Ted's: the risk of saying, doing, or even thinking something that would make them feel racist or like they could be seen as racist in interacting with the black passenger. It takes the perspective of the person whose actions one is trying to explain—the woman or minority taking the math test, for example, or in this case the perspective of the white passengers passing up the seat next to a black passenger. It assumes, in light of present-day norms of civility, that most of these passengers are invested in not appearing as racist. It further assumes that this investment, ironically, may lead them to avoid situations like the seat next to the black passenger or, more importantly, in light of the issues raised in the last chapter, to avoid teaching in a minority school or taking on a minority student mentee. In keeping Americans apart, this identity pressure might make people less interested in the strategies of intervention described in that last chapter, let alone in trying to apply them in a real-world setting.

This idea explains the Southwest Airlines First Class and suggests another "empirical question," which Philip Goff, a bright and energetic new graduate student in my lab who had long been thinking about these issues, wanted to take up. He moved me in that direction too. Our goal was to learn whether stereotype threat, in addition to its effects on performance, was also a common cause of tension between people from different groups in society, a tension that, presumably, could drive Americans apart.

But are Americans still being driven apart? When one thinks about factors that have traditionally isolated Americans from one another, many of them seem more muted today than in earlier times. American racial attitudes, for example, have grown consistently more accepting throughout the post–World War II era. Participation in virtually all aspects of American life, throughout this same period, has grown consistently more diverse—from the worlds of sports and entertainment to those of high-ranking CEO's and, of course, most recently in the presidency of the United States. The America projected in the media is enviably diverse. So were Americans still being driven apart? As Phil and I scanned the horizon for harder evidence on this question, images of intergroup harmony began to chip at the edges; even some major cracks began to emerge. And the cracks weren't all along racial lines.

In his recent book *On Paradise Drive*, the *New York Times* columnist David Brooks draws our attention to a general problem. We Americans are becoming more and more segregated into tinier and tinier enclaves of highly similar people, and this is happening around factors of much smaller significance than race. In large part, it reflects our pursuit of lifestyle and political preferences. Brooks takes the reader on a drive that begins in inner-city neighborhoods and progresses outward through the inner-ring suburbs, high-income professional neighborhoods, and immigrant enclaves, all the way to the "exurbs" and rural areas. He describes these communities as isolated "cultural zones." The people in them don't know much about people in the other zones, even when the zones border each other. In his words,

Human beings are capable of drawing amazingly subtle social distinctions and then shaping their lives around them. In the Washington, D.C., area, Democratic lawyers tend to live in suburban Maryland, and Republican lawyers tend to live in suburban Virginia. If you asked a Democratic lawyer to move from her $750,000 house in Bethesda, Maryland [in fall of 2003 prices], to a $750,000 house in Great Falls, Virginia, she'd look at you as if you had just asked her to buy a pickup truck with a gun rack and to shove chewing tobacco in her kid's mouth. In Manhattan the owner of a $3 million SoHo loft would feel out of place moving into a $3 million Fifth Avenue apartment.

Brooks further notes that Americans move a lot—that is, we're more likely than people in many other societies to uproot ourselves and relocate even to distant communities. This gives us lots of chances to choose where we live, which give us lots of chances to seek our own cultural zone, which, over time, makes these zones ever more like themselves, and ever more isolated from each other. In these ways, we're a nation of segregators.

And sometimes that segregation does involve race.

I occasionally think we Americans don't take enough credit for the significance of the civil rights movement—a public, in-law commitment to the ideal of a racially integrated society in virtually all of its aspects. I do not know of another society with such an explicit affirmation of this value, a major achievement of *Brown v. Board of Education*, the 1954 Supreme Court desegregation decision. But within two years of *Brown*, another Supreme Court decision granted school districts a more lenient standard of compliance. In the place of hard deadlines, it allowed "all deliberate speed." In 1974, the Court ruled against desegregation plans that spanned entire metropolitan areas as a means of integrating city and suburban schools. For predominantly minority cities with substantially white suburbs, this ruling made desegregation essentially impossible. Antibusing protests and court suits have persisted since the 1954 decision.

Over time, as the Harvard Civil Rights Project recently described, American schools have been resegregating. In the 185 school districts in the nation with enrollments of over 25,000 students, the vast majority were more racially segregated in 2000 than in 1986, often markedly so. For example, with the demise of the desegregation plan in Minneapolis, the average black student went to school with 33 percent fewer white students in 2000 than in 1986. Without desegregation plans, schools become as segregated as the neighborhoods that feed them. And those neighborhoods remain dramatically segregated, especially for whites. The 2000 census shows that the average white American lives in a neighborhood that is 80 percent white and 7 percent black, while the average black American lives in a neighborhood that is 33 percent white and 51 percent black. This holds for suburbs as much as for cities. If you wanted to rearrange most U.S. cities so that race played no role in where people lived, you would have to move 85 percent of the black population. Our history is still with us.

In the face of such data, Phil and I felt we'd answered our background question. Segregation, along with many dimensions of human difference, remains a major feature of American life. This includes racial segregation, television images of American society and presidential elections notwithstanding.

Still, one might ask, "So what?" Why worry about our segregating tendencies? It's a free country. If segregating by group identity causes no harm, why shouldn't we do it if we want to?

In this regard, the economist Glenn Loury, in a recent book,

The Anatomy of Racial Inequality, makes an interesting point. He says that whether or not one sees group segregation as problematic depends a lot on one's assumptions about the nature of people. One view is that people are more or less independent actors making free choices about opportunities that are more or less equally available to everyone in society. On that assumption, segregation shouldn't have much effect. The life chances you get are largely a matter of your own choice, determination, talent, and the like. So why worry about group segregation? It might mean you would be a little less cosmopolitan, but that wouldn't have much to do with how fair society is.

Another view, emerging especially in the social sciences, is that people, though capable of independent choice, do have a location in society; their lives are located somewhere in its social, economic, and cultural structures and in the networks of relationships that make up society. Being born into a low-income Appalachian family in the hills of eastern Kentucky is to take life on from a different location in society's opportunity structure than being born into a high-income family in the northern suburbs of Chicago. Different locations afford people different resources, different access to the "social capital" of skills, knowledge, opportunities, and life chances. Segregation affects location. When people are grouped or segregated on the basis of a characteristic like social class, race, or religion, it affects the resources and social capital that are available to them. As Loury puts it, "Opportunity travels along the synapses of these social networks" (p. 101). A fair amount of evidence supports him.

In the early 1970s, for example, the sociologist Mark Granovetter asked several hundred professionals in Newton, Massachusetts, how they got their jobs. Fifty-six percent pointed to a friend. Only nineteen percent responded to an ad, and only twenty percent got their job by directly applying. The sociologist Nancy DiTomaso recently expanded this line of investigation. For all of the jobs they ever had, she asked 246 people, twenty-five to fifty-five years old, in New Jersey, Ohio, and Tennessee, whether they'd been told about the job by someone they knew, whether someone "had put in a good word" for them, and whether they knew the person who hired them. For the average job, she found that 60 to 90 percent of her respondents had benefited from one or another of these forms of "social capital," and 98 percent of her respondents had benefited from at least one of these advantages for at least one of their jobs. Yet DiTomaso's respondents were largely unaware of their advantages: "[M]any interviewees said no one helped them. For example, a working class male from New Jersey who had gotten into the union through his father and then into a steadier job through help from a friend said, 'Did I earn it? Yeah, I worked for what I got. Definitely. Nobody gave me nothing. Nothing.' " When explaining our good fortune, we may remember our hard work and may be a bit too forgetful about the advantages of our social capital network.

And, of course, all networks are not created equal. It would surprise no one to find that people in wealthier locations and networks get easier access to better schooling, jobs, health care, and the like than people in less wealthy locations and networks. Think about the person I mentioned earlier who is born into a low-income Appalachian family in eastern Kentucky versus a person born into a high-income family in a wealthy suburb of Chicago. Think about Anatole Broyard when he was black versus when he was white. One way these people's locations differ is in the networks they offer, networks that vary in opportunities, access to skills and knowledge critical to success in society, access to people in the right places, and so on. This explains how seemingly ordinary associational preferences can have big effects. They influence who gets access to advantaging networks, and who doesn't.

This was Glenn Loury's reasoning. It led him to a surprising claim: the everyday associational preferences that contribute
to racially organized networks and locations in American life—
that is, racially organized residential patterns, schooling, friendship networks, and so on—may now be more important causes of
racial inequality than direct discrimination against blacks. He's not
announcing the end of racial discrimination. He's simply under-
lining the importance of preferences that organize blacks out of
networks and locations that could better their outcomes.

He cites examples of these preferences:

> [A]mong married persons 25–34 years old in 1990, some 70 per-
> cent of Asian women, 39 percent of Hispanic women, but only 2
> percent of black women had white Anglo husbands. . . . Racially
> mixed church congregations are rare enough to make front-page
> news. So culturally isolated are black ghetto-dwelling teenag-
> ers that scholars find convergence in their speech patterns over
> great geographic distances, even as this emergent dialect grows
> increasingly dissimilar from the speech of poor whites living but
> a few miles away. Childless white couples travel to Colombia and
> China in search of infants to adopt, while ghetto-born orphans
> go parentless. (p. 76)

As a further example of this, I can't help recalling the results
of the survey that I described in Chapter 2 in which the average
black student walking across the University of Michigan campus in
the early 1990s was found to have only two-thirds of a white friend
among his or her top six friends, while the number of black friends
that whites had was even smaller. Associations in the United States
clearly have a racial structure.

(Recall from the "minimal group" studies described in Chapter
4 that all groups have *in-group* associational preferences, the less

powerful and disenfranchised, as well as the more powerful and enfranchised. Thus, when getting into more advantaged networks would require relationships with people from an out-group—that is, when the less advantaged might have to develop relationships with the more advantaged out-group—these in-group preferences may get in the way. That said, almost by definition, the preferences of people already in advantaging networks will play a bigger role in determining who gets into them.)

As Phil and I sorted through this material, our suspicion that group prejudice wasn't the sole cause of group associational preferences grew stronger. We wondered whether identity threat didn't play a larger role in keeping Americans apart—in the Southwest Airlines First Class—than was recognized.

Yet we also knew that interracial interactions were often quite comfortable. Looking out my office window, we could see groupings of students as they came and went; they were often interracial and their interactions easy. Perhaps the topic of conversation made the difference. There are lots of things to talk about that would allow whites to feel little risk of confirming the racist stereotype—the fate of the school's basketball team, for example. Other topics would not assure such safety—for instance, the role of police in stopping black undergraduates in town, or a student's failure in tutoring an elementary school minority student—and that is where identity threat might come in, adding real tension to the interaction.

2.

But how to test all of this, how to test the role of identity threat in interracial interactions? We needed a way to measure the effect of identity threat on associational preference. Imagine, for example, that as a white person, you are waiting alone in a dentist's office as two black patients arrive and take seats near you. A conversation ensues. It starts as a commiserative chat about dental pain. Then it drifts toward politics and somehow finds its way to racial profiling, an issue of intense concern to your conversation partners. They believe they've experienced it. At this point, you're called into the doctor's office. But as you enter, the doctor leaves to finish a procedure with another patient. You return to the waiting room. Your former seat is taken. Two other seats are open, one next to your former conversation partners, who are still discussing racial profiling, and one farther away that would put you at a safe distance from this conversation.

Rejoining the conversation, as a white person, could put you under stereotype threat. That is, you could inadvertently say something on this charged topic that would cause you to be seen stereotypically. If identity threat of this sort affects associational preferences, then you might sit farther away from this risky conversation. But if identity threat has little effect on such preferences, you might just sit next to these guys and chat away.

Which seat do you take?

A situation like this might test whether identity threat, beyond any effect of prejudice, can affect one's preference to associate with other groups. A simple choice of seats would tell the story. Phil and I talked about many ways of setting this situation up in the laboratory. We gave several a dry run. Eventually we came to the following.

We brought white male Stanford University students into our laboratory, one at a time, explaining that as part of a study on social communication, they would have a conversation with two other students who were completing questionnaires in rooms down the hall. We took a Polaroid photograph of each participant and laid it on the table between Polaroids of their two conversation partners, to begin getting them acquainted. The photographs revealed that their conversation partners were black. Next, half of the participants learned that their conversation would focus on "love and relationships," and the other half learned that their conversation would focus on the more charged topic of "racial profiling."

This gave us two groups of white participants. One group expected to talk to two black guys about love and relationships—a topic that, in a pretest survey, male students rated as something they would feel comfortable talking about with people from different groups. They seemed to feel little risk of saying something on this topic that would cause them to be seen as racially prejudiced. The other group expected to talk to two black guys about racial profiling—a topic that the same pretest survey showed would make these students very uncomfortable, putting them under a stereotype threat much like that in my dental office example. Was this threat enough to affect the group preferences of these participants?

We measured these preferences in a simple way. After participants learned the topic of their conversation, the person conducting the experiment said that he would go down the hall to get the two other participants so that the conversation could begin. As he left, he pointed to three chairs clumsily grouped in the corner of the room and said, "Would you please do me a favor and arrange the three chairs for the conversation, and then take a seat in your chair?" The participant was then left to arrange the chairs. When this was done, the experiment was essentially over.

As you might surmise, our real interest was in how participants arranged the chairs, in particular, how close they placed their chair to the chairs of their two black conversation partners. These two distances—the distances between the participant's chair and the chairs of each of the two black conversation partners—were the basis of our measure of associational preference. We presumed that the greater these distances, like the choice of the more distant seat in the dental office, the less comfortable they anticipated being in the conversation.

If anticipating a conversation with two black students about racial profiling causes enough stereotype threat for whites to prefer less association with blacks, then expecting this conversation should lead white participants to place their chairs farther away from black partners than they would when expecting an innocuous conversation about love and relationships. They should behave like the white passengers avoiding the black passenger on Southwest Airlines flights. That is what happened. Participants expecting the love and relationship conversation grouped the three chairs close together. Those anticipating the racial profiling conversation, however, while grouping their two partners' chairs close together, put their own chair a distance away.

Interesting. But anybody might be uncomfortable talking to any stranger about racial profiling. It's a charged topic. Perhaps that is why participants seated themselves farther away from their partners when this was the conversation topic. To examine this possibility, we included two further groups of white male participants—one of which, just as before, expected a love and relationship conversation, and the other of which, just as before, expected a racial profiling conversation. But this time the photographs both groups saw at the outset of the experiment revealed that their conversation partners would be white, not black. Talking to two white students about racial profiling should not cause nearly as much stereotype threat as talking to two black students about racial profiling. The results were clear: white participants in both of these groups put the chairs close together regardless of the conversation topic. It wasn't just the racial profiling topic that led white participants to distance themselves from their black partners. But could we be sure that it was really fear of confirming the stereotype of whites as racist that was the cause of their distancing?

To find out, we measured what participants were thinking about just before they arranged the chairs. By means of the procedure that Josh and I had used earlier, we asked them to complete a list of eighty word fragments, ten of which could be completed as either a word related to the stereotype of whites as racists, or as a word not related to that stereotype. The fragment rac—t, for example, could be completed as either "racket" or "racist." Like a Rorschach test, this task measured what was just beneath a person's awareness. It showed something interesting. For participants expecting to talk to white partners, or to black partners about love and relationships, the number of fragments they completed with stereotype words did not increase with the distance they sat from the partners. But for participants expecting to talk to black partners about racial profiling, the more fragments they completed with stereotype words, the farther they sat from their partners.

This told us that the prospect of an interracial conversation on a racially sensitive topic made white participants mindful of the whites-as-racist stereotype. And the more mindful they were of this stereotype, the more they distanced themselves from black conversation partners. Worry about being stereotyped was driving them away.

But there was another explanation still. Remember the question about what caused the Southwest Airlines First Class—identity threat or old-fashioned prejudice? The same question was relevant here. Did white participants distance themselves from black partners when the topic was racial profiling because of identity threat, as we surmised, or because of prejudice? Perhaps the more racially prejudiced participants in this group sat farther away from their partners, reflecting their prejudice, and then had to worry the most about being seen as prejudiced.

We did another experiment. It used essentially the same procedures as the first, except this time, in a session twenty-four hours before the experiment began, we measured just how racially prejudiced our participants were. We measured both their conscious and unconscious prejudice. The conscious measure was the Modern Racism Questionnaire. The unconscious measure was the Implicit Attitude Test (IAT). The IAT measures one's unconscious or implicit attitude toward a given group, in this instance African Americans. It's built on the principle that it takes longer for us to say we recognize a weak mental association—for example, between George W. Bush and the pop star Michael Jackson, who are associated only by being public figures in the same era—than to say we recognize a strong mental association—for example, between Laurel and Hardy of the classic comedy team. So if we are faster at recognizing associations between blacks and negative things, such as between blacks and crime, than at recognizing associations between blacks and positive things, such as between blacks and career success, and if the reverse holds for our associations with whites, then we have an implicit negative association toward blacks. That is, our associations toward them are unconsciously more negative than our associations toward whites. (This interesting test, developed by the social psychologists Anthony Greenwald and Mahzarin Banaji, is available for readers to try out at www. implicit.harvard.edu.) Because the IAT relies on the time it takes people to react to stimuli that are rapidly presented on a computer screen, it is difficult to fake.

Our experiment, after taking these measurements, found the same thing as the first. White male participants expecting to talk about racial profiling seated themselves farther away from a black than from a white conversation partner. (Participants expected only one conversation partner in this experiment.)

Most important, the distance they put between themselves and their black partners was not greater for more prejudiced than for less prejudiced participants. It was true regardless of how prejudice was measured, consciously with the Modern Racism scale or subconsciously with the IAT. This is an illuminating finding. Prejudice had no effect on distancing in this experiment. Admittedly, our sample of elite college students wasn't a very prejudiced lot. Still, some participants tested more prejudiced than others, and these differences in prejudice had no effect on how close they sat to their black partner for the conversation on racial profiling.

What did affect how close they sat to their black partners was the same thing that affected it in the first experiment: how much they worried about confirming the whites-as-racist stereotype, a worry we measured in this experiment in exactly the same way we measured it in the first one, with word completions. When white male participants expected to talk to a black person about racial profiling, they feared confirming this stereotype, and the more they feared it, the farther away they sat.

It wasn't prejudice that caused them to sit farther from their black partners conversation. It was fear of being seen as racist— pure and simple. It was stereotype threat, a contingency of their white identities in that situation. It was probably this threat, too, rather than racial prejudice, that caused Ted's intense discomfort in his African American political science class, and that caused at least some of the white passengers to give Sheryll Cashin her Southwest Airlines First Class seat and that might make it difficult for white teachers to engage poor-performing minority students. Who needs the hassle?

Stereotype threat, then, is one way our national history seeps into our daily lives. That history leaves us with stereotypes about groups in our society that can be used to judge us as individuals when we're in situations where those stereotypes apply—in the seat next to a black person on an airplane or interacting with minority students, for example. The white person in that situation will not want to be seen in terms of the stereotype of whites as racially insensitive. And the black person, for his or her part, will not want to be seen in terms of the stereotypes about blacks as aggressive, or as too easily seeing prejudice, and so on. Fighting off these possible perceptions on a long airline flight—or more famously, perhaps, in a school cafeteria—could be more than either party wants to take on. They just want to have lunch or get to Cleveland. Avoidance becomes the simplest solution.

The stress of handling those stereotypes in public is perhaps a prime source of the "great American racial discomfort" or of the "great American discomfort with difference more generally," the discomfort that David Brooks tells us sends Americans into communities that are more and more organized around finer and finer "human distinctions." We may try to organize our residences, workplaces, and schools so as to achieve this avoidance. But with an increasingly diverse population, and the American commitment to fairness of access, avoidance will likely be a failing strategy. We can run, but can we hide?

Phil's and my reasoning thus far has a glum implication. Even if a magic wand waved away all of the prejudice in our society, there would still be pressures keeping us apart. As if that conclusion weren't glum enough, when this pressure is coupled with the American tendency to leave one's problems behind and move on (as Brooks notes, 16 percent of Americans move each year), you get a lot of energy in the direction of people segregating from one another.

3.

This is a fairly dark tunnel, but Phil and I, now joined by Paul Davies, whom I introduced earlier, did an experiment that sought light at the end of it—a mindset that could make it easier to approach people who are different from us. The idea, again, came from the work of Carol Dweck, whom I introduced earlier.

What white students perhaps worry about when talking to black students about racial profiling, we reasoned, following Carol's logic, is that a mistake in the conversation might confirm that they have a difficult-to-modify racism. They therefore shy away from the conversation. If so, we should be able to get them closer together if the conversation is presented as a learning opportunity. This would signal that the underlying skills involved are learnable, not immutable, and should take some of the apprehension out of the situation—enough, perhaps, that they could put their chairs closer together.

We ran the basic procedure of the experiment again. But this time, just before the participant was left to arrange the chairs for the conversation (as the experimenter ostensibly went down the hall to get a black conversation partner), the experimenter gave the participants an instruction. He said that tension was natural in a discussion of racial profiling, that it was difficult for everyone. He said they should treat the conversation as a learning experience— that is, try to learn what they could about the issue and, more generally, about how to talk about charged issues with people who might have differing perspectives.

Under this instruction, white male participants moved their chairs close to their black partner, as close as they were in any of the other groups in the experiment. What were they thinking about just before they arranged the chairs? The word fragments measure showed that, when they adopted a learning goal for their conversation, white participants no longer worried about being seen as racist. They now completed no more word fragments with stereotype-related words (words that meant racism) than participants who were not under stereotype threat.

Prejudice between groups is still a major cause of group segregation throughout the world. Simply teaching people to have learning goals when interacting with people from different groups may not, alone, cure all of these prejudices. No silver bullets exist in this business.

Still, this finding offers hope. When it is identity threat that keeps people apart and uncomfortable with each other, that prevents passengers from sitting next to each other on airplanes, that discourages students from taking courses with substantial numbers of minority students in them, or that may make teachers reluctant to approach some minority students, then learning goals might help. With a learning goal, mistakes become just mistakes, not signs of immutable racism.

Before we discovered Carol's idea of learning goals, we had some interesting failures. We had tried to find some instruction that would enable the participants expecting the challenging conversation to move their chairs closer. We tried first to assure them that they wouldn't be judged by what they said in the conversation, that they should feel free to speak their minds without fear of recrimination. It didn't work. Perhaps they didn't believe us. Those who anticipated talking to black partners about racial profiling still sat farther away. Next, we assured them that differences in perspective were valued, that a range of perspectives was appreciated in these conversations. This didn't work either. Chairs were still placed far apart, sometimes even farther apart than if we'd said nothing.

These strategies seemed reasonable to us. We'd gotten them from some of the diversity training programs we'd seen. We'd used them sometimes in our own classes. But they had an unforeseen consequence: the more we assured participants that we wouldn't hold their words against them, the more they feared we would. Paranoid, yes, but it is not entirely irrational in a psychology experiment, or in a diversity workshop, for that matter, where one can feel at risk of being judged. And that's the point. It's difficult to just assure away the stereotype threat that whites can feel in interracial situations, such as having a conversation with black colleagues about racial profiling, or that any group can feel in situations where negative stereotypes about them are relevant.

For assurances like these to work in classrooms, workplaces, or diversity workshops—or indeed for any group-relations technique to work—people have to be able to trust that, despite the relevance of a bad stereotype about their group, they won't be judged by it, that their goodness as human beings will be seen. Trust like that is hard to come by. Chapter 9 offers a number of what I hope are suggestive ways of achieving it. But here I stress again the value of learning goals. When interactions between people from different backgrounds have learning from each other as a goal, it eases the potential tension between them, giving missteps less significance. Trust is fostered.

Stereotype threat, then, is a general phenomenon. It happens to all of us, all the time. Negative stereotypes about our identities hover in the air around us. When we are in situations to which these stereotypes are relevant, we understand that we could be judged or treated in terms of them. If we are invested in what we're doing, we get worried; we try to disprove the stereotype or avoid confirming it. We present ourselves in counter-stereotypical ways. We avoid situations where we have to contend with this pressure. It's not all-determining, but it persistently, often beneath our awareness, organizes our actions and choices, our lives—like how far we walk down the isle of an airplane to find a seat, or how well we do on a round of golf, or on an IQ test. We think of ourselves as autonomous individuals. After all, we make choices. But we often forget that we make choices within contexts, always. And pressure tied to our social identities is a component of these contexts. This is difficult to appreciate by reflecting on our experience. And yet, as I've have urged throughout this book, it is precisely these pressures that make a social identity real for us.

Stereotype threat is a broad fact of life.

CHAPTER 11

Conclusion:
Identity as a Bridge Between Us

Since the election on November 4, 2008, of Barack Obama as president of the United States—the first African American president—there has been much talk about whether American society has entered a "postracial" era in which racial identity no longer plays an important role in our opportunities or in our relations with one another. It is a hope stirred by the election itself, and it extends to other group prejudices as well. At base, it is a hope that some essence in the American character has changed or evolved to the point of freeing us, going forward, from prejudice-based injustice, a problem left behind. Aristotle believed that objects fell at different speeds because they had internal essences, like "earthiness," that differed in how attracted they were to the earth and thus how fast they made the object fall to get there. We seem to think, too, that we can gauge our progress toward an identity-fair society by measuring an internal entity—intergroup prejudice—that we believe causes racial, gender, class, and other group injustices. If that barometer drops to zero, the idea goes, we would have a racially fair and identity-fair society, a level playing field, a postra-cial society. I, for one, would love to see that barometer fall to zero. But would that mean we'd have a postracial society?

The thrust of *Whistling Vivaldi* has been to offer a broadened view of what makes a social identity, like our race, important to us and to society. It isn't just the prejudicial attitudes of others toward the identity but also the contingencies that go with it in key settings. Prejudice matters. It can shape contingencies. But identity contingencies can profoundly affect a person—to the point of shaping her life—without her encountering a single prejudiced person along the way.

When I look over my life as an African American, I see improvements in the contingencies attached to that identity. The swimming pool restrictions of my youth are gone. So are the suf-focating limitations Anatole Broyard would have faced as a black man in New York City in the late 1940s. Things have gotten bet-ter. But remember, contingencies grow out of an identity's role in the history and organization of a society—its role in the DNA of a society—and how society has stereotyped that identity. In the case of race in the United States, that history and its legacies are still with us. The racial segregation of our schools, as we noted in the preceding chapter, is steadily increasing, not decreasing; reflecting the long history of racial subordination in the United States, the average black family today has only ten cents of wealth for every dollar of wealth the average white family has; and so on. As Wil-liam Faulkner famously said, "The past isn't dead and buried. In fact, it isn't even past."

In fact, the social psychological contingencies tied to race, while evolving, are nonetheless tenacious. Take the case of higher education. Until the 1960s the identity contingency that African Americans worried most about was that, on the basis of race, they couldn't get into most colleges and universities in the United States or that, if admitted, they would be in such small numbers and subjected to such segregating restrictions as to make the option highly unattractive. This contingency is hardly present at all in the lives of black college applicants today. Yet, as the research examined in these pages shows, the stereotype and identity threats that can arise in today's racially integrated colleges—especially those with an accumulation of identity-threatening cues—can be formidable, not as diminishing of life chances as the total exclusion of yesteryear, but an unfortunate suppression of human potential nonetheless.

Whites too, in these more diverse settings, may confront tenacious forms of identity threat. They regularly meet blacks and other minorities now, which means they regularly face the possibility of being judged in terms of negative stereotypes about whites—reactions to which we saw acted out in the experiments by Philip Goff, Paul Davies, and me described in Chapter 10.

This is why we don't yet have a postracial society. Our racial attitudes are indeed improving. Surveys show we oppose interracial marriage less; whites report being more comfortable working for a black boss; more Americans would be happy living next door to a person of a different race; and there is that election of an African American president. But it is contingencies in our lives, not racial attitudes alone, that count. And just because those contingencies are increasingly social psychological doesn't mean they're gone.

My mission in this book is to broaden our understanding of human functioning, to get us to keep in mind that, especially in identity-integrated situations, people are not only coping with the manifest tasks of the situation, but are also busy appraising threat and protecting themselves from the risk of being negatively judged and treated. Perhaps the chief discovery of our research is that this protective side of the human character can be aroused by the mere prospect of being negatively stereotyped, and that, once aroused, it steps in and takes over the capacities of the person—to such an extent that little capacity is left over for the work at hand. It shows that this side of the human character, aroused this way, affects our thoughts, emotions, actions, and performances in ways that have nothing to do with our internal traits, capacities, motivations, and so on, and that these effects contribute importantly to group differences in behavior, ranging from math performance to the interest shown in interracial conversations to playing golf. We could pry into the hearts and minds of people as deeply as science would allow looking for their true prejudices, and all the while miss the fact that on any given day their behavior toward blacks, for example, is determined mainly by a simple stereotype-driven predicament of identity that would affect most people who share their identity. Or we could give women a thousand tests to measure their capacity for mathematics and overlook that, in this society, from the time they first engaged mathematics they did so under the extra pressure of an identity threat that was especially strong at the frontier of their math skills and that made the whole activity seem like the unfriendly territory of another group. Or we could get times for the 100-meter dash from every major track meet in the world in search of white athletes' true running capacity and miss the reality that in the United States, ever since these runners began running fast, they did so under the almost complete societal consensus that running fast was the domain of another group.

This adds an ingredient to our understanding of group differences. It doesn't ignore the internal. It just broadens the palette of explanations. Without this broadened palette, you couldn't explain

- why changing the conception of a test from being diagnostic of ability to being a puzzle that is nondiagnostic of ability brings black performance to the same level as white performance on the Raven's Progressive Matrices IQ test, totally eliminating the typical racial gap in IQ scores;
- or why changing the definition of a golfing task from its being a measure of "natural athletic ability" to its being a measure of "sports strategic intelligence" completely reversed the performance ranking of white and black participants;
- or why reminding women math students about strong women role models just before they took a difficult math test could eliminate their typical underperformance on the test in relation to equally skilled men;
- or why describing a conversation with two African American students as a learning opportunity could get white male students to move their chairs closer for a conversation on racial profiling.

A central policy implication of the research discussed here is that unless you make people feel safe from the risk of these identity predicaments in identity-integrated settings, you won't succeed in reducing group achievement gaps or in enabling people from different backgrounds to work comfortably and well together. When this is not done, the protective side of the human character will hold sway over people and their resources. Addressing this need for safety won't completely remedy these problems. But the problems can't be remedied without attention to this need for safety. Along these lines, I've come to recognize that knowing how to address this side of the human character, especially in integrated settings, is an increasingly important skill for our teachers, managers, and leaders. It's not clear whether, without these skills, they could be effective in the increasingly diverse settings of our society.

This is where the practical lessons of *Whistling Vivaldi* come in. They constitute a beginning literature on what goes into that skill set. They offer a hopeful approach to the challenges I've outlined. Internal characteristics are hard to change; situational identity contingencies, the cues that signal them, and the narratives that interpret them are easier to change. That is illustrated by the practical findings emerging from this research in recent years:

- By changing the way you give critical feedback, you can dramatically improve minority students' motivation and receptiveness.
- By improving a group's critical mass in a setting, you can improve its members' trust, comfort, and performance in the setting.
- By simply fostering intergroup conversations among students from different backgrounds, you can improve minority students' comfort and grades in a setting.
- By allowing students, especially minority students, to affirm their most valued sense of self, you can improve their grades, even for a long time.
- By helping students develop a narrative about the setting that explains their frustrations while projecting positive engagement and success in the setting, you can greatly improve their sense of belonging and achievement—which if done at a critical time could redirect the course of their lives.

The effectiveness of these strategies is not an argument for neglecting structural and other changes that would help unwind the disadvantages attached to racial, gender, class, and other identities in our society. Such changes have to remain an important focus. But we can make a good deal of progress by addressing identity threat in our lives. And doing so is a big part of unwinding the disadvantages of identity. It may not take us all the way there.

But as I hope this book illustrates, it can take us closer than we may have recognized. And if we don't take that part of the journey, we won't get there at all.

* * * *

Still, we Americans are wary about focusing on identity. Could whatever gain it yields outweigh the divisiveness it might cause? Hasn't our use of race, for example, been one of our society's greatest shames? This is a big part of why we so want Obama's election to have marked the beginning of a postracial era—to put that shame behind us. It is perhaps ironic, then, in light of these hopes, that while Obama himself called for Americans of all identities to come together to build an era of progress, he didn't call for a postracial society or interpret his election as a sign that such a society had arrived. To the contrary, he stressed his racial and other identities, openly embraced them, wrote books about how important they were for him to understand and incorporate into his sense of self. He hungered for a strong, developed racial identity. Here he is in his own words on March 18, 2008, during his famous Philadelphia "race speech" in the heat of his campaign for the Democratic presidential nomination:

> I am a son of a black man from Kenya and white woman from Kansas. I was raised with the help of a white grandfather who survived a Depression to serve in Patton's Army during World War II and a white grandmother who worked on a bomber assembly line at Fort Leavenworth while he was overseas. I've gone to some of the best schools in America and lived in one of the world's poorest nations. I am married to a black American who carries within her the blood of slaves and slaveowners—an inheritance we pass on to our two precious daughters. I have brothers, sisters, nieces, nephews, uncles and cousins, of every race and every

hue, scattered across three continents, and for as long as I live, I will never forget that in no other country on Earth is my story even possible.

In this passage Obama is not hiding his racial identities but embracing them, not advocating a color-blind or postracial society but pointing to the many colors that make up this society and himself. He is putting identity and his multiple identities forward, using them as a bridge. In a society leery of identity, this could seem counterintuitive. Indeed, his staff advised him against this speech. Still, it may have gone farther than anything else he did to make nonblack Americans comfortable with him as a candidate and, eventually, as a president. It established a common ground between Obama and a huge swath of the American electorate. We all have identities, often many of them. And despite important differences between identities, a lot of the experience of having one identity is like the experience of having another identity. That he talked about his multiple identities enabled people to see this, to see into their own identities and what that understanding could tell them about the identity experiences of others. These stories of his bridged Obama to the multitudes. They enabled people to see themselves in him, a man who, without these stories about his identities, ironically would have been just a black man.

It also gave people, implicitly at least, a broader understanding of identities—that they are not rooted in unalterable essences that control the character of a person all the time. Important as identities are, people could see in Obama's experience that they don't capture or represent the whole person. They could see that identities are fluid, that their influence on us is activated by their situational relevance. It's a truth that many people sense in their own experience, and they apparently appreciated his having affirmed it. From this perspective, identity is less scary, less something to be wary of. In fact, exploring it might be helpful. Clearly Obama gained from exploring his identities; it gave him self-awareness and poise, insight and empathy into the circumstances of other people's lives, a connection to a great range of people, and the social competence to get things done. In his example, identity wasn't a source of balkanization and threat; it was a source of wisdom about the challenges of a complex and diverse society that ultimately made him the most suitable person to lead such a society. To the surprise of all, perhaps, it was his stress on identity, not his suppression of it, that made him a symbol of hope.

My hope for *Whistling Vivaldi* is that, in some small way at least, it will help to sustain that hope.

REFERENCES

CHAPTER ONE

Staples, B. Black Men and Public Space. (December 1986) *Harper's Magazine.*

Stone, J., Lynch, C. I., Sjomeling, M., & Darley, J. M. (1999). Stereotype threat effects on Black and White athletic performance. *Journal of Personality and Social Psychology* 77, 1213–1227.

CHAPTER TWO

Benbow, C. P., & Stanley, J. C. (1980). Sex differences in mathematical ability: Fact or artifact? *Science* 210, 1262–1264.

Benbow, C. P., & Stanley, J. C. (1983). Sex differences in mathematical reasoning ability: More facts. *Science* 222, 1029–1031.

Bentley Historical Library, University of Michigan. (2009). *University of Michigan Timelines: General University Timeline.* Retrieved from http://www.bentley.umich.edu.

Bentley Historical Library, University of Michigan. (2009). *University of Michigan Timelines: Diversity at the University of Michigan.* Retrieved from http://www.bentley.umich.edu.

Bombardieri, M. (2005, January 17). Summers' remarks on women draw fire. *Boston Globe*. Retrieved from http://www.Boston.com/boston-globe/.

Hemel, D. J. (2005, January 14). Summers' comments on women and science draw ire: Remarks at private conference stir criticism, media frenzy. *The Harvard Crimson*. Retrieved from http://www.thecrimson.com.

Hewitt, N. M., & Seymour, E. (1991). *Factors Contributing to High Attrition Rates Among Science, Mathematics, and Engineering Undergraduate Majors*. Report to the Alfred P. Sloan Foundation. Boulder, CO: Bureau of Sociological Research, University of Colorado.

Hewitt, N., & Seymour, E. (1997). *Talking about leaving: Why undergraduates leave the sciences*. Boulder, CO: Westview.

Jones, E. E., & Nisbett, R. E. (1972). The actor and the observer: Divergent perceptions of the causes of the behavior. In E. E. Jones, D. E. Kanouse, H. H. Kelley, R. E. Nisbett, S. Valins, and B. Weiner (eds.), *Attribution: Perceiving the causes of behavior*. Morristown, NJ: General Learning Press.

Peters, W. (producer and director). (1970). *Eye of the storm*. New York: ABC News, ABC Media Concepts.

Spencer, S. J., Steele, C. M., & Quinn, D. (1999). Stereotype threat and women's math performance. *Journal of Experimental Social Psychology* 35, 4–28.

Summers, L. (2005). Remarks at NBER Conference on Diversifying the Science & Engineering Workforce. Retrieved from http://www.president.harvard.edu/speeches/2005/nber.html.

Wilson, W. J. (1987). *The truly disadvantaged: the inner city, the underclass and public policy*. Chicago: University of Chicago Press.

Wilson, W. J. (ed.) (1993). *The ghetto underclass*. Newbury Park, CA: Sage.

Chapter Three

Allport, G. (1958). *The nature of prejudice.* Garden City, NY: Doubleday.

NBA Seattle Supersonics. Retrieved from: www.nba.com/sonics/new/00401097.html.

Scott, D. M. (1997) *Contempt and pity: Social policy and the image of the damaged Black psyche.* Chapel Hill: University of North Carolina Press.

Steele, C. M., & Aronson, J. (1995). Stereotype threat and the intellectual test performance of African Americans. *Journal of Personality and Social Psychology* 69, 797–811.

Chapter Four

Brooks, Tim. (2004). *Lost sounds: Blacks and the birth of the recording industry, 1890–1919.* Chicago: University of Illinois Press, 174.

Comer, J. (1988). Educating poor minority children. *Scientific American* 259, 42.

Comer, J. (2000). *Child by child: The Comer process for change in education.* New York: Teachers College Press.

Gates Jr., H. L. (1997). The passing of Anatole Broyard. In *Thirteen ways of looking at a Black man.* New York: Random House, 180–214.

Glass, I. (2000, July 28). *This American Life: Americans in Paris,* Episode 165. Washington D.C.: National Public Radio.

Maalouf, A. (1998). Deadly identities. Retrieved from http://www.aljadid.com/essays/DeadlyIdentities.html.

Maalouf, A. (2001). *In the name of identity: Violence and the need to belong.* New York: Arcade Publishing.

Mitgang, H. (1990, October 12) Anatole Broyard, 70, book critic and

editor at the *Times*, is dead. *New York Times*. Retrieved from http://
www.nytimes.com/1990/10/12/obituaries/anatole-broyard-70-book-
critic-and-editor-at-the-times-is-dead.html.

Rowland, Mabel. (1923). *Bert Williams, son of laughter*. New York: The
English Crafters.

Tajfel, H. (1957). Value and the perceptual judgement of magnitude.
Psychological Review 64, 192–204.

Tajfel, H., Billig, M., Bundy, R., & Flament, C. (1971). Social categoriza-
tion and intergroup behavior. *European Journal of Social Psychology*
1, 149–178.

Tajfel, H., & Turner, J. C. (1979). An integrative theory of intergroup
conflict. In W. G. Austin & S. Worchel (eds.), *The social psychology
of intergroup relations*. Monterey, CA: Brooks/Cole, 33–47.

Tajfel, H., & Turner, J. C. (1986). The social identity theory of intergroup
behavior. In S. Worchel & W. G. Austin (eds.), *Psychology of intergroup relations*. Chicago: Nelson, 7–24.

CHAPTER FIVE

Aronson, J., Lustina, M. J., Good, C., Keough, K., Steele, C. M., &
Brown, J. (1999). When White men can't do math: Necessary and
sufficient factors in stereotype threat. *Journal of Experimental Social
Psychology* 35, 29–46.

Croizet, J.-C., & Claire, T. (1998). Extending the concept of stereotype
and threat to social class: The intellectual underperformance of students from low socioeconomic backgrounds. *Personality and Social
Psychology Bulletin* 24, 588–594.

Drake, S. C., & Cayton, H. R. (1945). *Black metropolis: A study of Negro
life in a northern city*. New York: Harcourt Brace.

Hess, T. M., Auman, C., Colcombe, S. J., & Rahhal, T. A. (2002).

The impact of stereotype threat on age differences in memory performance. *Journal of Gerontology: Psychological Sciences* 57B, P3–P11.

McIntyre, R. B., Paulson, R. M., & Lord, C. G. (2002). Alleviating women's mathematics stereotype through salience of group achievement. *Journal of Experimental Social Psychology* 39, 83–90.

Pittinsky, T. L., Shih, M., & Ambady, N. (1999). Identity adaptiveness: Affect across multiple identities. *Journal of Social Issues* 55, 503–518.

Shih, M., Pittinsky, T. L., & Ambady, N. (1999). Stereotype susceptibility: Identity salience and shifts in quantitative performance. *Psychological Science* 10, 80–83.

CHAPTER 6

Fullilove, R. E., & Treisman, P. U. (1990). Mathematics achievement among African American undergraduates at the University of California, Berkeley: An evaluation of the Mathematics Workshop Program. *Journal of Negro Education* 59 (3), 463–478.

Jones, V. D. (2009). The pressure to work harder: The effect of numeric underrepresentation on academic motivation. Unpublished doctoral dissertation, Stanford University.

Leavy, W. (April 1997) 1947–1997: The 50th anniversary of the Jackie Robinson revolution. *Ebony*, 52.

Nussbaum, A. D., & Steele, C. M. (2007). Situational disengagement and persistence in the face of adversity. *Journal of Experimental Social Psychology* 43, 127–134.

O'Brien, L. T., & Crandall, C. S. (2003). Stereotype threat and arousal: Effects on women's math performance. *Personality and Social Psychology Bulletin* 29, 782–789.

Treisman, P. U. (1985). *A study of mathematics performance of Black students at the University of California, Berkeley.* Unpublished report.

Treisman, P. U. (1992). Studying students studying calculus: A look at the lives of minority mathematics students in college. *College Mathematics Journal* 23, 362–372.

CHAPTER SEVEN

Ben-Zeev, T., Fein, S., & Inzlicht, M. (2005). Arousal and stereotype threat. *Journal of Experimental Social Psychology,* 41 (2), 174–181.

Blascovich, J., Mendes, W. B., Hunter, S. B., Lickel, B., & Kowai-Bell, N. (2001). Perceiver threat in social interactions with stigmatized others. *Journal of Personality and Social Psychology* 80, 253–267.

Blascovich, J., Spencer, S. J., Quinn, D. M., & Steele, C. M. (2001). African Americans and high blood pressure: The role of stereotype threat. *Psychological Science* 13 (3), 225–229.

Croizet, J. C., Desprès, G., Gauzins, M., Huguet, P., & Leyens, J. (2003). *Stereotype threat undermines intellectual performance by triggering a disruptive mental load.* Unpublished manuscript, Université Blaise Pascal, Clermont-Ferrand, France.

Dutton, D. G., & Aron, A. P. (1974). Some evidence for heightened sexual attraction under conditions of high anxiety. *Journal of Personality and Social Psychology* 30, 510–517.

James, S. A. (1993). The narrative of John Henry Martin. *Southern Cultures* 1 (1), 83–106.

James, S. A. (1994). John Henryism and the health of African-Americans. *Culture, Medicine, and Psychiatry* 18, 163–182.

James, S. A., Hartnett, S. A., & Kalsbeek, W. D. (1983). John Henryism and blood pressure differences among black men. *Journal of Behavioral Medicine* 6 (3), 259–278.

James, S. A., Keenan, N. L., Strogatz, D. S., Browning, S. R., & Gar-
rett, J. M. (1992). Socioeconomic status, John Henryism, and blood
pressure in black adults: The Pitt county study. *American Journal of
Epidemiology* 135 (1), 59–67.

James, S. A., LaCroix, A., Kleinbaum, D. G., & Strogatz, D. S. (1984).
John Henryism and blood pressure differences among black men ii:
The role of occupational stressors. *Journal of Behavioral Medicine* 7
(3), 259–275.

Mendes, W. B., Blascovich, J., Lickel, B., & Hunter, S. (2002). Challenge and threat during social interaction with white and black men.
Personality and Social Psychology Bulletin 28, 939–952.

Schmader, T., & Johns, M. (2003). Convergent evidence that stereotype
threat reduces working memory capacity. *Journal of Personality and
Social Psychology* 85, 440–452.

Steele, C. M., Spencer, S. J., & Aronson, J. (2002). Contending with
group image: The psychology of stereotype and social identity threat.
In M. P. Zanna (ed.), *Advances in experimental social psychology*. San
Diego, CA: Academic Press, 34, 379–440.

CHAPTER EIGHT

Allmendinger, J. M., & Hackman, J. R. (1993). *The more, the better?
On the inclusion of women in professional organizations*. Report No.
5, Cross-National Study of Symphony Orchestras, Harvard University.

Ashe, A., & Rampersad, A. (1993). *Days of grace*. New York: Knopf.

Davies, P. G., Spencer, S. J., & Steele, C. M. (2005). Clearing the air:
Identity safety moderates the effects of stereotype threat on women's
leadership aspirations. *Journal of Personality and Social Psychology*
88 (2), 276–287.

Inzlicht, M., & Ben-Zeev, T. (2000). A threatening intellectual environment: Why females are susceptible to experiencing problem-solving deficits in the presence of males. *Psychological Science* 11, 365–371.

Krendl, A. C., Richeson, J. A., Kelley, W. M., & Heatherton, T. F (2008). The negative consequences of threat: a functional magnetic resonance imaging investigation of the neural mechanisms underlying women's underperformance in math. *Psychological science: a journal of the American Psychological Society*, 168–175.

Murphy, M. M., & Steele, C. M. (in prep). *The importance of context: Understanding the effects of situational cues on perceived identity contingencies and sense of belonging.* Unpublished manuscript, Stanford, CA.

Murphy, M. M., Steele, C. M., & Gross, J. J. (2007). Signaling threat: Cuing social identity threat among women in a math, science, and engineering setting. *Psychological Science* 18 (10), 879–885.

O'Connor, S. D. (2003). *The majesty of the law: Reflections of a Supreme Court justice.* New York: Random House.

Purdie-Vaughns, V., Steele, C. M., Davies, P. G., Ditlmann, R., & Crosby, J. R. (2008). Social identity contingencies: How diversity cues signal threat or safety for African Americans in mainstream institutions. *Journal of Personality and Social Psychology* 94, 615–630.

Totenberg, Nina. (2003, May 14) Sandra Day O'Connor's supreme legacy: First female high court justice reflects on 22 years on bench. *All Things Considered.* Retrieved at http://www.npr.org/templates/story/story.php?storyId+1261400.

CHAPTER NINE

Ambady, N., Shih, M., Kim, A., & Pittinsky, T. L. (2001). Stereotype susceptibility in children: Effects of identity activation on quantitative performance. *Psychological Science* 12, 5, 385–390.

Aronson, J., Fried, C., & Goode, C. (2002). Reducing the effects of stereotype threat on African-American college students by shaping theories of intelligence. *Journal of Experimental Social Psychology* 38, 113–125.

Bok, D., & Bowen, W. (1998). *The shape of the river.* Princeton, NJ: Princeton University Press.

Cohen, G. L., Garcia, J., Apfel, N., & Master, A. (2006, September 1). Reducing the racial achievement gap: A social-psychological intervention. *Science* 313, 1307–1310.

Cohen, G. L., Steele, C. M., & Ross, L. D. (1999). The mentor's dilemma: Providing critical feedback across the racial divide. *Personality and Social Psychology Bulletin* 25, 1302–1318.

Cole, S., & Barber, E. (2003). *Increasing faculty diversity: The occupational choices of high-achieving minority students.* Cambridge, MA: Harvard University Press.

Dweck, C. S. (2006). *Mindset: The new psychology of success.* New York: Random House.

Dweck, C. S. (2007). The secret to raising smart kids. *Scientific American Mind* 12, 36–40.

Massey, D. S., Charles, C. Z., Lundy, G., & Fischer, M. J. (2002). *The source of the river: The social origins of freshman at America's selective colleges and universities.* Princeton, NJ: Princeton University Press.

Muzzatti, B., & Agnoli, F. (2007). Gender and mathematics: Attitudes and stereotype threat vulnerability in Italian children. *Developmental Psychology* 43 (3), 747–759.

Steele, C. M., Spencer, S. J., Hummel, M., Carter, K., Harber, K., Schoem, D., & Nisbett, R. (1997). *African-American college achievement: A wise intervention.* Unpublished manuscript, Stanford University.

Steele, D. M., Steele, C. M., Markus, H. R., Lewis, A. E., Green, F., &

Davies, P. G. (2008). *How identity safety improves student achievement.* Manuscript submitted for publication.

Walton, G. M., & Cohen, G. L. (2003). Stereotype lift. *Journal of Experimental Social Psychology* 39, 456–467.

Walton, G. M., & Cohen, G. L. (2007). A question of belonging: Race, social fit, and achievement. *Journal of Personality and Social Psychology* 92, 82–96.

Walton, G. M., & Spencer, S. J. (2009). Latent ability: grades and test scores systematically underestimate the intellectual ability of negatively stereotyped students. *Psychological Science* 20 (9), 1132–1139.

CHAPTER TEN

Brooks, David. (2004). *On Paradise Drive: How we live now (and always have) in the future tense.* New York: Simon & Schuster.

Cashin, S. (2004). *The failures of integration: How race and class are undermining the American dream.* New York: Public Affairs.

DiTomaso, N. (2006, August 11). Social Capital: Nobody Makes It on Their Own. Paper presented at the annual meeting of the American Sociological Association, Montreal Convention Center, Montreal, Quebec, Canada Online. Retrieved from http://www.allacadmic.com/meta/p103086_index.html.

Goff, P. A., Steele, C. M., & Davies, P. G. (2008). The space between us: Stereotype threat and distance in interracial contexts. *Journal of Personality and Social Psychology* 94, 91–107.

Granovetter, M. S. (1973). The strength of weak ties. *American Journal of Sociology* 78 (6), 1360–80.

Granovetter, M. S. (1974) *Getting a job: A study of contacts and careers.* Cambridge, MA: Harvard University Press.

Greenwald, A. G., McGhee, D. E., & Schwartz, J. L. K. (1998). Measuring individual differences in implicit cognition: The Implicit Association Test. *Journal of Personality and Social Psychology* 74, 1464–1480.

Greenwald, A. G., Nosek, B. A., & Banaji, M. R. (2003). Understanding and using the Implicit Association Test: I. An improved scoring algorithm. *Journal of Personality and Social Psychology* 85, 197–216.

Lee, C., & Orfield, G. (2007, August 29). School desegregation. Harvard Civil Rights Project. Retrieved from http://www.civilrightsproject .ucla.edu/research/deseg/reversals_reseg_need.pdf.

Loury, G. (2002). The anatomy of racial inequality. Cambridge, MA: Harvard University Press.

Chapter 11

Obama, B. Speech on Race (2009, March 18). *New York Times*.

INDEX

ABC News, 27–28
ability:
  as expandable, 168–69, 178–79, 181
  as innate (fixed), 83, 168–69
academic underachievement:
  of blacks, 19–22, 23, 25–26, 30,
    49–59, 101–8, 111, 112–13,
    156–59, 165–68, 186
  critical mass in remediation of,
    143–44, 159
  cultural capital and, 22, 47, 156, 158
  family role in, 182, 182n–83n
  of female math students, see women,
    math underachievement of
  identity contingencies in, 2–3, 158,
    173, 182
  identity threats and, 15, 80, 156, 159
  inclusive narratives in remediation of,
    165–68, 181, 216
  intervention strategies and, 166–67,
    181, 186–90
  in K through 12 students, 129–90
  of minorities, 22, 30, 43, 156–59,
    171, 173, 184–90
  skill and knowledge deficits in, 48,
    57–58, 157, 181–82
  socioeconomic class and, 15, 158,
    182
  stereotype threats as cause of, 12–13,
    30–34, 36–43, 48–59, 80,
    88–98, 101–14, 116–26, 143–
    44, 156–59, 165–90, 212–15
  see also underperformance

actor's perspective, 18, 21, 24
Advanced Placement (AP) exams,
    188n
affirmative action:
  lasting societal impact of, 155–56
  Supreme Court rulings on, 134–35,
    137–38
African American political science class,
  McDougal in, 2–3, 4, 85–89,
    126, 132–33, 139, 140–41, 144,
    148, 154, 163–64, 192, 205
African Americans:
  athletic ability as positive stereotype
    of, 9, 75, 97, 215
  changing contingencies of, 212
  financial inequality of, 212
  ghettoization of, 25
  hypertension in, 128–33
  intelligence stereotype threat and,
    133n, 153
  in Paris, 80–82, 83
  "passing" by, 64–68, 82–83, 197
  psychic damage as explanation of poor
    outcomes for, 46–47
  segregation and, see segregation, racial
    underperformance as downwardly
    recursive for, 176
  violence stereotype threat and, 6–7,
    11
African American students, 17–29
  critical feedback and, 162–64
  as downwardly constituted, 25–26
  group-learning workshops for, 112–13

African American students (continued)
  intelligence stereotype threat and,
    10–11, 49–59, 60, 87, 88, 89,
    99, 101–3, 106–7, 117, 153–54,
    167–69, 213, 215
  isolated study habits of, 101, 103, 113
  over-efforting by, 101–8, 112–13
  SATs and, 19–20, 185
  and sense of not belonging, 20,
    24–25, 103, 165–66
  separation of academic and social
    lives by, 101–2
  social networks of, 21–22, 23, 26
  strong, effect of stereotype threats on,
    49–50, 89, 138
  underachievement of, 19–22, 23,
    25–26, 30, 49–59, 101–8, 111,
    112–13, 156–59, 165–68, 186
age, aging:
  mental capacity stereotype and, 68,
    70, 96–97
  and sense of not belonging, 139
  as social identity, 70
Agnoli, Franca, 170
alcohol addiction, 29
Allmendinger, Jutta, 136–37
Allport, Gordon, 46, 89
All Things Considered, 134–35
Ambady, Nalini, 92–93, 170
analogy, as route to empathic insight,
    60
Anatomy of Racial Inequality, The
    (Loury), 195–96
Andrew Mellon Foundation, 155–57
angular gyrus, 125
anxiety, see stress reactions
Apfel, Nancy, 174
Aron, Arthur, 114–16
Aronson, Joshua, 48–56, 90, 95, 96,
    116–17, 168–69, 172–77,
    178–79, 203
Ashe, Arthur, 140, 146
Asian American students:
  integration of academic and social
    lives of, 100–101

positive math stereotype of, 90–93,
    170
associational preferences, 197–99
  experiments in, 200–209
  identity threat and, 199–210
  minimal group effect and, 76–79,
    198–99
athletic ability, stereotype threats and,
    4, 8–11, 14, 60–61, 97, 121,
    214, 215
avoidance, stereotype threat and, 54,
    206, 207, 209

Baker, Josephine, 80
Baldwin, James, 80
Banaji, Mahzarin, 204
Barber, Elinor, 156
Bell Curve, The (Herrnstein and Mur-
    ray), 153
Bellow, Saul, 64
belonging, sense of, 20, 24–25, 103
  age and, 139
  identity threats and, 143–46, 152–53,
    160–61, 173
  in newsletter experiment, 145–47
  positive narratives for, 165–68, 181,
    216
Benbow, Camilla, 34–35
Ben-Zeev, Avi, 120, 143
bias:
  minimal group effect and, 76–79,
    198–99
  in observer's perspective, 18
  in standardized tests, 187–88
  as unavoidable, 14
Billig, Michael, 76–79
bipolar disorder, 70–71
Black Metropolis (Cayton and Drake),
    86–87
blackness, as situational contingency, 87
blacks, see African Americans
Blascovich, James, 118–19
blood pressure:
  stereotype threats and, 118–19, 121,
    132, 149

see also hypertension
Bok, Derek, 155–56
"bougie girls," "project girls" vs., 80, 82
Bowen, Bill, 155–57
Boys High School, Brooklyn, 65
brain activity, stereotype threat and, 15, 125
Bristol, University of, 76
Brooklyn College, 65
Brooks, David, 193–94, 206
Brown, Joseph, 55, 90
Brown v. *Board of Education,* 194
Broyard, Anatole, 64–67, 68, 74, 82–83, 197, 212
Broyard, Paul, 65
Broyard, Sandy, 83
Bundy, M. G., 76–79

California, University of, at Berkeley, 99–100
Capilano Bridge experiment, 114–16, 118, 120, 126
Cashin, Sheryll, 191–92, 205
Cayton, Horace, 86–87
Chicago, Ill.:
  city politics in, 86–87
  Hyde Park neighborhood in, 6–7, 10, 11
  segregation in, 1–4, 52, 74, 212
child-centered teaching, 181
"choking," in athletes, 124
civil rights movement, 194
Claire, Theresa, 95–96
class, socioeconomic, 19
  academic underachievement and, 15, 158, 182
  in social organization, 95–96, 141, 212, 216
  in stereotype threat, 95–96, 121
classroom performance, stereotype threats and, 4, 13, 86–89, 173
Clermont-Ferrand, University of, 95–96
Clinton, Hillary, 141
cloaking threats, 177, 189
cognitive load:

heartbeat interval and, 122–23
  see also mental resources
Cohen, Geoffrey, 161–66, 171–77, 187
Cole, Stephen, 156
Coleman Report, 182*n*–83*n*
College and Beyond study, 155–56
colleges and universities:
  affirmative action and, *see* affirmative action
  athletic vs. academic commitment at, 155
  culture of, 25
  low-income students at, 155
  minorities at, 16–26, 28, 43, 151*n*, 155, 167
  minority faculty at, 25, 151*n*, 159
  social organization of, 19, 21–22, 23, 26, 28, 167
  see also academic underachievement; African American students
Comer, James, 75–76
comfort levels, stereotype threats and, 4, 13
Contempt and Pity (Scott), 46
Crandall, Christian, 109–10, 188*n*
critical feedback, stereotype threat and, 162–64, 216
critical mass of minorities, 133*n*, 135–38, 140–41, 142, 151*n*, 216
  and academic achievement, 143–44, 159
  in newsletter experiment, 145–47
Croizet, Jean-Claude, 95–96, 121–22
Crosby, Jennifer Randall, 143
Cross, William, 1
cues, in identity threats, 70, 75–76, 138–51, 177
  density of, 140, 171
  to diversity, 141
  incidental, 148–50, 153, 165
  to marginality, 140–41, 173
  as offset by identity safety cues, 147–48, 150, 151*n*, 160–61, 179–80, 184, 215
  to prejudice, 141, 142

cues, in identity threats (continued)
    reduction of, 183–84, 216
    and sense of belonging, 143–46,
        152–53, 160–61, 173, 180, 181
    vigilance as aroused by, 148–51, 160,
        214
cultural capital, as lacking in under-
    achievers, 22, 47, 156, 158
cultural zones, 193–94, 198, 206
culture, intersubjectivity and, 5, 42,
    59–60

Danaher, Kelly, 188n
Davies, Paul, 143, 144, 179–80, 207–9,
    213
discrimination, racial:
    associational preferences vs., 198–99
    in employment, 3, 25, 26
    social identity and, 74
    see also prejudice
DiTomaso, Nancy, 196–97
diversity, cues to, 141
diversity policy, and sense of belonging,
    146–47
downwardly constituting factors, 25–26,
    28, 30
Drake, St. Clair, 86–87
Dutton, Donald, 114–16
Dweck, Carol, 168, 172–77, 178, 207,
    208

Ebony, 108
Edgecombe County, N.C., 131
Educational Testing Service (ETS), 188n
Elliott, Jane, 26–28, 30, 34, 40
emotions, limited self-awareness of,
    114–18
empathic insight, analogy as route to, 60
empirical research, 14, 37, 40, 52, 84,
    89, 94, 143, 155
employment, racial discrimination in, 3
environment, modification of, 179–84
expatriation, 80–82, 83
"Eye of the Storm, The" (ABC News),
    27–28

Failures of Integration, The (Cashin),
    191–92
family environment, academic
    underachievement and, 182,
    182n–83n
Faulkner, William, 212
favoritism, see bias
Flament, Claude, 77–79
fMRI imaging, 124–25
Four Seasons (Vivaldi), 6, 7
France, French:
    prejudice in, 81
    social class in, 95–96, 121
Fried, Carrie, 168–69
friendships:
    as de facto segregation, 25, 167
    interracial, 21–22
    see also social organization

Garcia, Julio, 172–77, 187
Gates, Henry Louis, Jr., 64, 83
gender:
    achievement gaps and, 12, 15
    as social identity, 70, 92, 212, 216
    in social organization, 141
    stereotypes about, 138, 140, 142, 144
    see also women
genocide, identity threat and, 72
Ginsburg, Ruth Bader, 135–38, 140,
    142, 144, 147, 150
Glass, Ira, 79–80
Goff, Philip, 193, 195, 199, 200–209,
    213
golf experiment, 8–11, 97, 121
Good, Catherine, 90, 168–69, 172–77,
    178–79
Graduate Record Exam (GRE), 188n
Granovetter, Mark, 196
Gratz v. Bollinger, 134–35, 137
Great Migration, 25, 65
Green, Francis, 179–80
Greenwald, Anthony, 204
Greenwich Village, 66
Gross, James, 148–50
Grutter v. Bollinger, 134–35, 137–38

Hackman, Richard, 136–37
happiness, effect of chronic identity
    threats on, 127
Harber, Kent, 166–67
Harvard Civil Rights Project, 195
Harvard University, 36
    math stereotype experiment at, 90–92
health, racial disparities in, 128–33
heartbeat interval, cognitive load and,
    122–23
heart rate, stereotype threat and, 149
Heatherton, Todd, 124–25
Heckman, James, 182n–83n
Herrnstein, Richard, 153
Hess, Thomas, 96–97
Hewitt, Nancy, 31
history, as downwardly constituting
    factor, 28
Hopkins, Nancy, 36
housing, segregation of, 3, 66, 156,
    195
"How Much Can We Boost IQ and
    Scholastic Achievement?" (Jen-
    sen), 153
Hummel, Mary, 166–67
hypertension in blacks, 128–33
    socioeconomic oppression as factor
    in, 130, 131

identity:
    gender, see gender
    racial, see race
identity, social, 3–4, 14, 59–62, 67, 68
    as adaptations to situational con-
        tingencies, 79–82, 83–84, 87,
        126–27, 210, 212, 218
    class and, 95–96, 141, 212, 216
    as defined by threatening contingen-
        cies, 73–76
    equality in, 211–12, 216
    examples of, 70–71
    as fluid, 218–19
    neutral and positive contingencies of,
        73, 74–75
    see also social organization

identity contingencies:
    academic underachievement and,
        2–3, 158, 173, 182
    as affecting life outcomes, 4, 14,
        61–62, 144–45, 210, 212, 216
    innate abilities and, 83
    limited self-awareness of, 121,
        144–45
    as modifiable, 79–84, 92–94, 151
    as physical constraints, 5, 69, 74
    race and, 2–4, 14, 66–69, 79–81, 87,
        153, 205
    as situational, 69, 79–82, 83–84, 91,
        93, 126, 138–39, 210, 218
    stereotype threats as, 5, 11–12, 52,
        59–61, 67, 68, 69, 80, 88–89,
        183–84, 212
    underperformance and, 2–3, 4,
        59–62, 63, 80, 93, 125–26, 154,
        158
    use of term, 68
    see also identity threats; stereotype
        threats
identity integration, 139, 142
identity safety:
    cues for, 147–48, 150, 151n, 160–61,
        179–80
    narratives for, 154, 179, 181, 184,
        216
    skill sets for creation of, 215–16
identity threats:
    academic underachievement and, 15,
        80, 156, 159
    chronic, 126, 127–33
    as cloaking, 177, 189
    cues in, see cues, in identity threats
    de facto segregation and, 192–93
    as diffuse, 71, 76, 154, 177, 189
    narratives and, 154, 163–69, 173–74,
        179, 181
    power of, 76–79, 88–89, 138–39,
        154
    as preoccupying, 71–72, 73, 75, 76,
        120–21, 125–26, 139–40, 141,
        154

identity threats (*continued*)
  vigilance and, 75, 125–26, 139–40,
    141, 148–51, 160, 164*n*, 167,
    176, 213–14
  violence as response to, 72–73
  see also identity contingencies; stereo-
    type threats
Implicit Attitude Test (IAT), 204–5
imposter syndrome, 153
individualism, 137
  as American creed, 4, 61
intelligence stereotype threat, 10–13, 49,
    60, 67, 88, 89, 93, 99, 106–7,
    117, 133*n*, 153–54, 213, 215
  experiments in, 50–59, 167–69
intergroup tensions, stereotype threats
    and, 13, 15, 68–69, 193,
    199–210
intersubjectivity, stereotype threats and,
    5, 42, 59–60
intervention strategies, academic under-
    achievement and, 166–67, 181,
    186–90
intervention studies:
  college-level, 166–67, 187
  in K through 12 schools, 171–79,
    182, 183*n*, 184, 187
In the Name of Identity (Maalouf), 72–73
Inzlicht, Michael, 143

Jackson, Michael, 65
James, Sherman, 127–32
Jeff (college student), 102–3, 111
Jensen, Arthur, 153
John Henry (folklore char.), 129
John Henryism, 130–33, 148
Johns, Michael, 123–24, 125
Jollet, Mikel, 55–59
Jones, Edward, 18
Jones, Valerie, 110
Josephs, Robert, 29

Kansas, University of, 109
Keller, Johannes, 170
Kelley, William, 124–25

Keough, Kelli, 90
King, Martin Luther, Jr., 26–27
Krendl, Anne, 124–25

Latinos, academic underachievement of,
    22, 30, 156–59
learning, stereotype threats as impedi-
    ment to, 86–87
learning opportunity scenario, stereotype
    threats defused in, 207–9, 215
left parietal cortex, 125
Lewis, Amanda, 179–80
Lord, Charles, 94
Los Angeles, Calif., intelligence stereo-
    type experiment in, 55–59
Loury, Glenn, 195–96, 198
low self-esteem, *see* self-doubt
Lustina, Michael, 90

Maalouf, Amin, 72–73
McDougal, Ted, 2–3, 4, 85–89, 126,
    132–33, 139, 140–41, 144, 148,
    154, 163–64, 192, 205
McIntyre, R. B., 94
Majesty of the Law, The (O'Connor), 135
marginality, cues to, 140–41
Markus, Hazel, 179–80
Martin, John Henry, 128–33
Massachusetts Institute of Technology,
    35–36
Massey, Douglas, 156–59
Master, Allison, 174
math, Treisman's workshops for teaching
    of, 99–100, 112–13
math ability:
  of Asian Americans, 90–93
  of white males, stereotype threat and,
    90–92
  of women, *see* women, math under-
    achievement of
mean arterial blood pressure (MAP),
    stereotype threats and, 118–19,
    121
memory, working, rumination and,
    123–24, 132

Mendes, Wendy, 119
mental health status, as identity threat,
    70–71, 75
mental resources:
    of older persons, 68
    stereotype threat and allocation of,
        12–13, 43, 110–11, 121–27,
        164*n*, 167, 176, 181–82
Michigan, University of:
    affirmative action lawsuits against,
        134–35, 137–38
    math stereotype experiments at,
        32–34, 38–40, 48, 49–51, 58
    minorities at, 16–22, 167, 187
Mills, Charles, 25
mind-body relationship, 148
minimal group effect, 76–79
minorities:
    academic underachievement of,
        22, 30, 43, 156–59, 171, 173,
        184–90
    assumed vs. real prejudice against,
        75–76
    on college faculties, 25, 151*n*, 159
    as college students, 16–26, 28, 43,
        151*n*, 155, 167
    critical mass of, *see* critical mass of
        minorities
    and sense of not belonging, 20,
        24–25, 103, 142–44
    see also race; *specific minorities*
Modern Racism Questionnaire, 204–5
motivation, as lacking in underperform-
    ers, 22, 46
Murphy, Mary, 143, 148–50
Murray, Charles, 153
Muzzatti, Barbara, 170

narratives:
    identity threats and, 154, 163–69,
        173–74, 179, 181
    self-affirming, 29, 172–77, 179, 181,
        216
National Basketball Association, 11
nationality, as social identity, 70

National Public Radio, 134–35
Native Americans, academic under-
    achievement of, 22, 30, 158
New School for Social Research, 66
newsletter experiment, 145–47
New Yorker, The, 64
New York Times, 64, 66
New York Times Book Review, 64
New York University, 66
Nisbett, Richard, 18, 21, 166–67
North Africans, 81
North Carolina, University of, Medical
    School of, 128
North Carolina State University, 96–97
Nussbaum, David, 105–8

Obama, Barack, 141, 211, 213, 217–19
O'Brien, Laurie, 109–10
observer's perspective, 17–18, 21, 22,
    24, 45, 46–47, 52, 57, 63
O'Connor, Sandra Day, 134–38, 139–40,
    142, 144, 147, 148, 150–51
Ohio State University, author as graduate
    student at, 152–54, 159–61,
    163–64, 165, 182
older persons, *see* age, aging
On Paradise Drive (Brooks), 193–94
opportunity, as affected by social organi-
    zation, 196–99
Ostrom, Thomas, 159–61, 163–64
over-efforting, 98, 101–8, 112–13
    experiment in, 106–7

Paris, African American expatriates in,
    80–82, 83
"passing," 64–68, 82–83, 197
Paulson, R. M., 94
Pennsylvania, University of, 156
personal adequacy, affirmation of, *see*
    self-affirmation
perspective, *see* actor's perspective;
    observer's perspective
physiological cost, *see* stress reactions
Pitt County, N.C., 131
Pittinsky, Todd L., 92–93

political affiliation, as social identity, 70
Porter, Carol, 104–5, 107
prefrontal cortex, 125
prejudice:
    as cause of segregation, 208
    cues to, 141, 142
    real vs. assumed, 75–76
    social identity and, 74, 211–12
    stereotype threats vs., 164*n*, 192, 199,
        203–6, 212
    trust and, 164*n*
    underperformance as independent of,
        42
    see also discrimination, racial
Princeton University, 156
    golf experiment at, 8–11, 97, 121
    organic chemistry class at, 104–5,
        107–8
profession, as social identity, 70
"project girls," "bougie girls" vs., 80, 82
psychology students, as less intelligent
        than science students, 122–23
Purdie-Vaughns, Valerie, 143, 145–48,
        150, 174–77, 187

Quinn, Dianne, 118–19

race:
    achievement gaps and, 15
    in American history, 28, 69, 80–81,
        193, 205–6, 217–19
    associational preferences and,
        198–210
    health disparities and, 128–33
    identity contingencies and, 2–4, 14,
        66–69, 79–81, 92–93, 205, 212,
        216
    as social identity, 70, 87, 92–93, 153,
        167
    social organization and, 19, 21–22,
        23, 25, 26, 80–81, 95, 167
    see also minorities; *specific minorities*
racism, 26
    as stereotype threat, 2–3, 4, 24,
        86–89, 200–208, 213

Radcliffe Institute, 69–70
Raven's Progressive Matrices IQ test,
        122, 215
Remote Association Task, 118–19
Richeson, Jennifer, 124–25
Richmond, Calif., 179–80
Robinson, Jackie, 108
Ross, Lee, 162–63
rumination, stereotype threat and,
        121–24, 126–27, 132
Rustin, Bayard, 86

San Francisco State University, 120
SATs, 12, 50*n*, 185, 187, 188
    of female math students, 31–32
    as predictor of academic success,
        19–20
    see also standardized tests
Schmader, Toni, 123–24, 125
schools, K through 12:
    black students in, 55–59
    de facto segregation in cafeterias of,
        68–69, 141
    environmental modification and,
        179–84
    inadequate funding of, 25
    intervention strategies for, 181
    intervention studies in, 171–79, 182,
        183*n*, 184, 187
    quality of instruction in, 177, 182,
        183*n*
    segregation of, 3, 47, 158, 194–95,
        212
    skill and knowledge deficits in,
        181–82
    stereotype threat and, 55–59,
        169–90
    teacher practices in, 179–80
Science, 35
science students, as more intelligent
        than psychology students,
        122–23
scientific inquiry:
    bias as constrained by, 14
    choice points in, 29

empirical testing in, 14, 37, 40, 52,
     84, 89, 94, 143, 155
Ostrom's dedication to, 160–61
replication in, 175
Scott, Daryl, 46
Seattle Supersonics, 44–45, 47, 52, 57,
     59
segregation:
   by cultural zones, 193–94, 198, 206
   prejudice as cause of, 208
   social identity and, 74
segregation, racial:
   author's encounters with, 1–4, 52, 74,
     212
   of housing, 3, 66, 156, 195
   of schools, 3, 47, 158, 194–95, 212
segregation, racial, de facto:
   in friendships, 25, 167
   identity threats and, 192–93
   in school cafeterias, 68–69, 141
self-affirmation, 29, 172–77, 179, 181,
     216
   moderators of, 176–77
self-doubt, as cause of underperfor-
     mance, 22, 42, 46, 89, 91–92,
     94, 124, 138, 157, 176
self-esteem:
   in-group favoritism and, 78–79
   threats to, 172–73
sexual orientation, as social identity, 70
Seymour, Elaine, 31
Shape of the River, The (Bowen and
     Bok), 155–56, 157
Shih, Margaret, 92–93
situational contingencies, 69, 79–82,
     83–84, 91, 93, 126, 138–39,
     210, 218
skill frontiers, 41, 108–9, 111
social capital, 196–97
social organization:
   associational preferences in, 197–99
   class in, 95–96, 141, 212, 216
   of college students, 21–22, 23, 25,
     167
   cultural zones in, 193–94, 198, 206

as downwardly constituting factor, 28
   gender in, 141, 212
   identities and, see identity, social
   mobility and, 194, 206
   opportunities as affected by, 196–99
   race in, 3, 21–22, 23, 25, 26, 67,
     80–81, 95, 141, 167, 212
   segregation in, 196–97
   see also culture; segregation
social progress, stereotype threat as
     hindrance to, 15
socioeconomic disadvantage, 47
Source of the River, The (Massey et al.),
     157
South, American, white use of violence
     in, 85–86
"Southwest Airlines First Class,"
     191–92, 199, 202, 203, 205
Spencer, Steven, 29–34, 36–43, 49,
     50–51, 116–17, 118–19, 144,
     166–67, 184–89
standardized tests:
   bias in, 187–88
   stereotype threats and, 4, 12–13,
     50–51, 58–59, 120–21, 148,
     180, 184–90
   as underestimating potential of stereo-
     typed students, 184–90
Stanford University, 48
   associational preference experiments
     at, 200–209, 213
   intelligence stereotype experiments at,
     50–55, 58, 167–69
   math and science stereotype experi-
     ments at, 90–92, 149–50
   over-efforting experiment at, 106–7
Stanley, Julian, 34–35
Staples, Brent, 6–7, 10, 11
Steele, Claude M.:
   in childhood encounters with segrega-
     tion, 1–4, 52, 74, 212
   as Ohio State graduate student,
     152–54, 159–61, 163–64, 165,
     182
Steele, Dorothy, 179–80

stereotype threats:
  academic underachievement and,
      12–13, 30–34, 36–43, 48–59,
      80, 88–98, 101–14, 116–26,
      143–44, 156–59, 165–90,
      212–15
  age, 139
  athletic ability, 4, 8–11, 14, 60–61,
      97, 121, 214, 215
  avoidance and, 54, 206, 207, 209
  blood pressure and, 118–19, 121, 132
  brain activity and, 125
  classroom performance and, 4, 13,
      86–89, 173
  comfort levels and, 4, 13
  critical feedback and, 162–64, 216
  definition of, 5
  as downwardly recursive process, 176
  emotional investment and effect of,
      56–59, 62n, 113, 126, 130–33,
      138, 209
  environmental modification and,
      179–84
  failed strategies for defusing of, 208–9
  as fear of confirming negative ste-
      reotypes, 5, 52–53, 56, 58, 83,
      88–89, 98, 108–9, 111–12, 121,
      123, 125, 130, 131, 205–6, 207,
      213–14
  as general phenomena, 49, 52, 60, 88,
      94, 95, 97–98, 209–10
  as generating search for external
      explanations, 54
  Ginsburg's experience of, 136, 138,
      140, 150
  as hindrance to social progress, 15
  as identity contingencies, 5, 11–12,
      52, 59–60, 67, 68, 69, 80, 93,
      183–84, 212
  intelligence, 10–13, 49–59, 60, 67,
      87, 88, 93, 99, 101–3, 106–7,
      117, 133n, 153–54, 167–69,
      213, 215
  intergroup tensions and, 13, 15,
      68–69, 193, 199–210

  intersubjectivity and, 5, 42, 59–60
  K through 12 students and, 169–90
  learning as impeded by, 86–87
  learning opportunity scenario in
      defusing of, 207–9, 215
  McDougal's experience of, 2–3,
      4, 85–89, 126, 132–33, 139,
      140–41, 144, 148, 154, 163–64,
      192, 205
  math ability, 12, 34, 38–40, 48,
      49–51, 83, 90–92, 116–17, 124,
      144
  memory impairment, 43, 96–97
  mental resources diverted by, 12–13,
      43, 110–11, 121–27, 132, 164n,
      167, 176, 181–82
  O'Connor's experience of, 135–36,
      137, 138–40, 142, 144, 147,
      148, 150–51
  over-efforting as response to, 98,
      101–8, 112–13
  as performance boosters, 109–10,
      112
  prejudice vs., 164n, 192, 199, 203–6,
      212
  prior susceptibility as factor in, 89,
      90, 157
  racism, 2–3, 4, 24, 86–89, 200–208,
      213
  reduction of, 7, 11, 13, 15, 38, 43,
      51, 94, 98, 133n, 151, 173–84,
      207–9
  rumination induced by, 121–24,
      126–27, 132, 164n
  self-affirmation and, 29, 173–77, 179,
      181, 216
  and sense of belonging, see belonging,
      sense of
  skill frontiers and, 41, 108–9, 111
  socioeconomic class and, 95–96,
      121
  standardized tests and, 4, 12–13,
      50–51, 58–59, 120–21, 148,
      180, 184–90
  Staples's experience of, 6–7

stress reactions (physiological cost) and, 13, 43, 111–12, 118–21, 148–50
strong students as especially vulnerable to, 41, 49–50, 54–59, 89, 92, 94, 138
underperformance and, 15, 29–34, 36, 40, 48, 49, 80, 84, 90–92, 132, 154, 189–90
violence, 24
weak students as minimally affected by, 57, 62n
stigmatization, see stereotype threats
Stone, Jeff, golf experiment of, 8–11, 97
Stoutemeyer, Kirsten, 94
stress reactions:
limited self-awareness of, 115–18, 121, 126–27
stereotype threats and, 13, 43, 111–12, 118–21, 148–50
study habits, 101–3, 113
Summers, Larry, 35–36
Supreme Court, U.S.:
affirmative action rulings of, 134–35, 137–38
women justices on, 134–38, 139–40, 142, 144, 147, 148, 150–51
sweating, stereotype threat and, 149
Symes, S., 130
symphony orchestras, women in, 136–37

Tajfel, Henri, 76–79
terrorism, identity threat and, 72
Texas, University of, 99–100
Texas Assessment of Academic Skills (TAAS), 178–79
This American Life, 79–80
Totenberg, Nina, 134–35
Treisman, Philip Uri, 99–105, 107, 111, 112–13
trust:
and assumed vs. actual prejudice, 164n
critical feedback and, 162–63
in good teacher practices, 181, 183n

narratives of, 166–67, 181, 183n
in newsletter experiment, 145–47
Turner, John, 78

underperformance:
concentration of factors in, 26
as downwardly recursive, 176
generalization of empirical data on, 49–50, 52, 95, 97–98
identity contingencies and, 2–3, 4, 59–62, 63, 80, 154
as independent of prejudice, 42
observer-perspective explanations for, 22, 45, 46–47, 52, 57, 63
self-doubt as cause of, 22, 42, 46, 89, 91–92, 94, 124, 138, 157, 176
stereotype threats and, 15, 29–34, 36, 40, 48, 49, 80, 84, 132, 154, 189–90
and susceptibility to stereotype threat, 89, 90, 157
see also academic underachievement; specific skills and settings
United States:
population mobility in, 194, 206
as "postracial" society, 211–12, 213, 217
racial history of, 28, 69, 80–81, 193, 205–6, 211–12, 213, 217–19

ventral anterior cingulate cortex, 126
vigilance, identity threats and, 75, 125–26, 139–40, 141, 148–51, 160, 164n, 167, 176, 213–14
violence:
in black stereotype threat, 6–7, 11
white Southerners' use of, 85–86
Vivaldi, Antonio, 6, 7

Walton, Greg, 164–66, 184–89
war, identity threat and, 72
Washington, University of, 16, 29
well-being, sense of, effect of chronic identity threats on, 127
"White Like Me" (Gates), 64

whiteness, as situational contingency, 87
whites:
    athletic stereotype threat and, 8–10,
        14, 60–61, 97, 214, 215
    racist stereotype threat and, 2–3, 4,
        24, 86–89, 200–208, 213
    Southern, violence used by, 85–86
    study habits of, 101
Wilkens, Lenny, 44–45, 47
Williams, Bert, 84, 151
Wilson, William Julius, 25
women:
    negative stereotypes about, 142, 144
    over-efforting by, 108
    positive role models for, 94, 215
    as Supreme Court justices, 134–38,
        139–40, 142, 144, 147, 148,
        150–51
    in symphony orchestras, 136–37
    in technology, 110–11
women, math underachievement of, 22,
    214

biological differences as explanation
        for, 34–36, 40–41
    experiments in, 32–34, 38–40, 48,
        49–51, 58, 90–92, 149–50
    in K through 12 students, 170,
        178–79
    multiple factors in, 41
    and sense of belonging, 143–44
    skill frontiers and, 41, 108
    stereotype threat and, 12, 30–34, 36,
        38–40, 48, 49–51, 58, 60, 83,
        89, 92–93, 94, 99, 116–17, 121,
        124, 144, 170, 178–79, 215
    in strong students, 41, 49, 89, 138
    vs. women in English studies, 31–32,
        33
word completion tests, 53, 203, 205
working memory, rumination and,
        123–24, 132
Wright, Richard, 80